DEGAS LETTERS

W9-ADU-200

1. SELFPORTRAIT IN A SOFT HAT

EDGAR GERMAIN HILAIRE

D E G A S

LETTERS

EDITED BY

MARCEL GUERIN

With 27 Illustrations

B R U N O   C A S S I R E R

O X F O R D

TRANSLATED FROM THE FRENCH BY
MARGUERITE KAY

Printed in Great Britain by
ROBERT MACLEHOSE & CO. LTD., GLASGOW

Published 1947 *by*
BRUNO CASSIRER, PUBLISHERS, LTD.
31 PORTLAND RD., OXFORD

INTRODUCTION

A certain picture of Degas exists, almost legendary, mythical; it is the artist as a recluse, voluntarily leading a churlish life, warding off with his rapid and trenchant replies the indiscretions of the world and of people, even contact with them. Of this picture which actually was known, admired from a distance and feared from close to by those of Degas' contemporaries who thought that they knew him, but in reality did not know him at all, of this picture then there will be no more than an occasional glimpse in distant outline in the letters reunited in this volume. So let the reader be warned, let him not search for what he will not find in these pages. The centre here is not the Degas known to the writers, it is Degas himself, different from what he seemed.

Not without earnest consideration have his friends decided to assemble the letters written to them, to publish his correspondence. To reveal the intimate side of this man who had lived so jealous of his intimacy, was that not a betrayal of his intentions, a going against them? They did not think so! This secret with which Degas covered his life, he even applied it to his work, which he included in his intimacy. Always working, searching, almost always dissatisfied, he kept the greater part of it hidden in boxes out of which he scarcely ever took anything—and when he did so, with what severity of choice—except what he was forced to sell to enable him to live. Well, this œuvre, so often sad in character (and

5

he knew this better than anyone) it has been disclosed in its entirety. And so why keep the letters hidden, why make an exception of them when they reveal so much nobility? The reason for such an exception does not exist.

The Degas who is revealed here is the artist and the friend. The artist following a double dream of increasingly exigent accuracy and ever freer invention; the artist, artisan bound up with the realization of the work of the material quality of line and colour as much as with the magic quality of the whole. The indefatigable friend: to attend a funeral, to clasp a hand Degas took the train and travelled 15 hours and all beneath the cover of a mask of insensibility, beneath uncouth habits, which did not touch the depths. 'My hard heart melts all the same', he wrote about a stricken friend. But the mask was immediately resumed. 'What is this I hear' he cried one day bursting like a whirlwind upon a young and charming woman, one of his favourite hostesses, and calling out from the doorstep 'what is this! I hear you are saying everywhere that I am not bad, that people are mistaken in me! If you take that away what will be left to me?'—There will be left, there is left the man who wrote these letters.

Degas was he a letter writer? Certain pages in the present volume (for instance the letter to Froelich) prove so conclusively.[1] But to develop this talent of his two things were lacking: First time, he worked too much, and secondly sight: suffering, threatened he husbanded it for the studio. He wrote with his eyes half closed without seeing; which explains the frequent slips of the pen which

[1] These words brought me a sharp reply from George Moore. See appendix p. 236 sq. for the letters he wrote to me.

6

are not spelling mistakes.[1] Restricted in this manner he finally came to feel a certain distaste. 'I do not like writing' we read in a letter to Henri Rouart; and elsewhere he insists: 'I do not like writing, I only know how to talk, even when I have nothing to say'. It seems to us that in this disgust was more of weariness than of instinctive distaste. Degas was not one of those oral improvisers whose inspiration dries up at the sight of a pen. He spoke as he wrote, with the same sparkling and savoury power, the same clarity. Down to the last brief, sad notes of the final years, there still persists the old vivacity, the character, the line, the manifest signs of a gift used only when occasion demanded.

DANIEL HALÉVY

A considerable number of letters which have come to light since the first edition was published have been included, the letters have been re-arranged, and the notes revised and amplified. Three appendixes have been added containing letters from Degas' friend, Paul Poujaud to Marcel Guérin, from George Moore to Daniel Halévy, and notes made by D. H. after discussions with Degas.

MARCEL GUÉRIN

Dates, if not noted by Degas himself, have been printed in italics.

Only short notes have been added at the foot of the pages. Fuller explanations follow the text on p. 259 so as not to disturb the reader, who may not require them.

[1] These slips of the pen have been disregarded in the translation unless, as in the case of names of people or places, the word is the same in English and French. (M.K.).

7

CONTENTS

1

To Tissot

Paris, 30 Sept. 1871

Tissot,[1] why the devil did you not send me a line? They tell me you are earning a lot of money. Do give me some figures.

Within the next few days I may possibly make a flying visit to London with Achille.[2] But it is not yet certain. In the meanwhile honour me with a few details.

Mlle Strauss, whom you have neglected shamefully, wishes to be remembered to you. She has broken off her association with Mme Moreau and, after a brief spell of real hardship, that she could describe to you in detail if you took the trouble to go and see her, she is carrying on the business. You, it appears, could help her in this. She was preparing to extol your talent. She now thinks that through the connections you have made you could praise hers and make use of it. With regard to the death of Moreau she and his wife still doubt it.

Stevens never stops telling us that he is doing masterpieces and that this year he will easily exceed one hundred thousand francs.

I have seen something new of Manets, of medium size, well finished, done lovingly, in a word a change. What talent the fellow has.

[1] See annotations, p. 259.
[2] Achille De Gas, younger brother of Edgar.

11

I exhibited my *Orchestre de l'Opéra* in the rue Lafitte. The crowd . . . no, I shall say nothing: that would be Courbet.

I have just had and still have a spot of weakness and trouble in my eyes. It caught me at Chateau by the edge of the water in full sunlight whilst I was doing a water-colour and it made me lose nearly three weeks, being unable to read or work or go out much, trembling all the time lest I should remain like that.[1]

Give me some idea how I too could gain some profit from England. Goodbye, answer my letter. Jacquemart has just returned and was worried about you.

And what about the marriage?

I very much doubt whether Reitlinger will help this month. Anyway I have got almost everything out of him. He gave me an I.O.U. for three months for one part.

Detaille wanted to buy your house. Rumour had it you wished to sell it. Is it true?

Warmest greetings,

DEGAS

Remember me to Whistler, Legros. Astruc has this moment come to fetch me to see his lovely water colours.

[1] See annotations, p. 259 No. 2.

2

To Desire Dihau[1]

DE GAS BROTHERS, NEW ORLEANS

11 Nov. *1872*

My dear Dihau,

Thank you for your good letter. It is the first. Already they are forgetting me over there. Please forgive me; I should have guessed your promptness in writing to me and have at least written to you from New York. All the same I am expecting a second edition from you before you receive this.

We had an excellent journey. Ten days at sea is a long time; particularly on an English boat where there is so much reserve. If we could have taken the French boat of the 10 October we should have found some travelling company in which the women at least would have helped us to kill time. No more seasickness for the one than for the other and for my part an appetite such as I had never known and which had every appearance of permanency; it is falling off here; I eat next to nothing. 30 hours wait at New York. Left Thursday at 6 o'clock, we were due at New Orleans at 11 o'clock on Monday with several hours wait at Louisville, as fresh and fatter than when we left. You must have heard of the Wagons Lits; but you have never seen one, you have never travelled in one and so you cannot imagine what this marvellous invention is like: You lie down at night in a proper bed. The carriage which is as long as at least 2 carriages in France is transformed

[1] See annotations, p. 260.

13

into a dormitory. You even put your shoes at the foot of the bed and a kind negro polishes them whilst you sleep. —What luxuriousness you will say. No, it is a simple necessity. Otherwise it would be impossible to undertake such journeys at a stretch. And then the ability to walk all round your own coach and the whole train, to stand on platforms is immensely restful and diverting. Everything is practical and very simply done here, so simply that the trains leave almost without warning.—Well I was with René[1] who is from these parts and I did not miss anything.

Lord how we laughed at your story of the innovations and of the manager of the crémerie.[2] You gave us a real treat, and being so far from Paris makes it all the more precious.—What part did my dear little Maury play among the cooks? that of Mathilde by any chance? If it really is that, she deserved what you said of her.—The rascal, not one word from her yet.

So the good Simon has not yet had my letter written at sea and posted at the tip of Ireland where we caught the mail for Europe. This letter posted there on the 13th should have reached her on the 15th or 16th. Mlle Malot[3] has just replied to a letter from René posted in the same way. I thanked her warmly for all her goodness to me. Why does she wish me more calmness in my ideas? Am I then an unusually excitable person?

I shall beg forgiveness from my Lille friends when I am back. There is a touch of malice in their reply and that does not do any harm. If you have not already been to

[1] René De Gas, 1845–1920, the artist's youngest brother.
[2] A small restaurant.
[3] Mlle Malot, dancer at the opera. Degas did two portraits of her which are among his best: Coll. J. E. Blanche (pastel) and II. Vente Degas, no. 48.

14

Lille by January I shall go with you and assume an attitude of courteous submission.

You will certainly have seen my cruel friend again[1] and I am sure that a letter from you is already on the way. Every morning at my brother's office I await the arrival of the mail with more impatience than is altogether fitting.[2]

Ah! my dear friend, what a good thing a family is; we were met at the station. My uncle looked at me over his spectacles; my cousins, their six children were there. The surprise that René had planned for them by not saying that I was with him failed; as there had been some talk of yellow fever still persisting at New Orleans he had telegraphed to Achille asking if that meant there would be any danger for a stranger and the cat was out of the bag. All day long I am among these dear folk, painting and drawing, making portraits of the family. My poor Estelle, René's wife, is blind as you know.[3] She bears it in an incomparable manner; she needs scarcely any help about the house. She remembers the rooms and the position of the furniture and hardly ever bumps into anything. And there is no hope!—Pierre, René's son, is superb; he is so self-possessed and the mixture of English and French is so quaint!—Odil, his little girl, is 12 to 15 months old. Jane, the eldest, his wife's daughter, has a real feeling for music; she is beginning to solfa in the Italian solfeggio. There is also a little Carrie, daughter of Mathilde, the youngest of my cousins. Mathilde also decided to have another

[1] This probably refers to Mlle Marie Dihau, sister of Désiré Dihau. See annotations, p. 260

[2] This is the office represented by Degas in his famous picture in the musée de Pau.

[3] A portrait of her is in Washington. (Rewald, Degas and his family in New Orleans, Gazette des Beaux Arts 1946, p. 105.)

young boy called Sydney and a little brat of 2 months called Willy.—This whole band is watched over by negresses of different shades.[1] We are awaiting the arrival, today or tomorrow, by the ship Le Strassbourg, of a French nurse whom René engaged in Paris.

Mlle Sangalli[2] will doubtless remain all the winter. I shall thus be able to enjoy her on my return. What you tell me about Vittoq (?) delights me.

Give my regards to our friends of the orchestra. If you see Gard[3] put in a word for me with this tyrant.

Greetings to Piot,[4] Demarquette, Ziegler etc. and to the distinguished patroness.—What you tell me about Madier gives me great pleasure. Here in the French company we have a Mlle Winke (?) who was a dancer at the Français and whom Madier wanted me to meet in Paris because of my dance picture and of the roguish air of the lady. I regret very much not being quite introduced.

Goodbye, believe in my friendship.—If you see Clotilde ask her to write and tell me what is happening at home.

DEGAS

[1] The picture no. 25 of the first Vente Degas, representing children on the steps of a country house, was certainly painted at New Orleans.

[2] Rita Sangalli, famous opera dancer who created the role of Sylvia in Léo Delibes' ballet, *Sylvie ou la Nymphe de Diane*.

[3] Gard, producer of dance at the Paris opera; he figures in the picture *l'Orchestre* (Louvre).

[4] Piot-Normand, artist and friend of Degas. He figures in the same picture.

16

2. JAMES TISSOT

3. ITALIAN BOY

3

To Tissot

DE GAS BROTHERS, NEW ORLEANS

19 Nov. 1872

My dear Tissot, what do you say to the heading? It is the paper of the firm. Here one speaks of nothing but cotton and exchange. Why do you not speak to me of other things? You do not write to me. What impression did my dance picture make on you, on you and on the others?—Were you able to help in selling it? And the one of the family at the races, what is happening to that? Oh how far from so many things one is here.

Excellent journey. New York has some charming spots. We spent scarcely two days there. Monet and Pissarro would make mis talk (sic) there. What a degree of civilization! Steamers coming from Europe arrive like omnibuses at the station. We pass carriages, even trains on the water. It's England in her best mood.

After four days in the train we arrived at New Orleans. You cannot imagine a wagon-lit sliping car (sic). A real dormitory. Behind curtains one can undress down to one's chemise if one wants to, and then climb into a real apple-pie bed. Everything is done simply and except for some points of taste, one says to oneself: it's true, it's just what I needed. The practical Englishman seems to be bristling with mania and prejudices. One feels at once that there is rivalry with the mother country.—Mother country? But Germans are arriving in their thousands, half the shops in Broadway have names like Eimer and Wolf, Schumaker and Vogel, etc. Texas is full of Germans. The other day

17

a French maid whom René had engaged before leaving arrived on a small German boat. In the hold, like niggers in Biard's pictures, were 651 German emigrants fleeing the Vaterland, misery and a new war with Russia or fair France. Fair France still has a quarter of a foot in Louisiana. The Creole cannot measure strength with the Yankee.

Villas with columns in different styles, painted white, in gardens of magnolias, orange trees, banana trees, negroes in old clothes like the junk from *La Belle Jardinière* or from Marseilles, rosy white children in black arms, charabancs or omnibuses drawn by mules, the tall funnels of the steamboats towering at the end of the main street, that is a bit of local colour if you want some, with a brilliant light at which my eyes complain.

Everything is beautiful in this world of the people. But one Paris laundry girl, with bare arms, is worth it all for such a pronounced Parisian as I am. The right way is to collect oneself, and one can only collect oneself by seeing little. I am doing some family portraits; but the main thing will be after my return.

René has superb children, an excellent wife who scarcely seems blind, although she is, almost without hope, and a good position in business. He is happy, it is his country perhaps even more than France.

Achille has one foot over there and the other here. I still do not know and he does not know himself if he will come with me in January.

And you, what news is there since the 700 pounds? You with your terrible activity would be capable of drawing money out of this crowd of cotton brokers and cotton dealers, etc. I shall not attempt to earn anything here.

May this letter of mine cross something from you. Did

18

you get my photographs? Here I have acquired the taste for money, and once back I shall know how to earn some I promise you.

If you see Millais, tell him I am very sorry not to have been able to see him and tell him of my appreciation for him. Remember me to young Deschamps, to Legros, to Whistler who has really found a personal note in that well-balanced expression, mysterious mingling of land and water.

I have not yet written to Manet and naturally he has not sent me a line. The arrival of the mail in the morning really excites me. Nothing is as difficult as doing family portraits. To make a cousin sit for you who is feeding an imp of two months is quite hard work. To get young children to pose on the steps is another job of work which doubles the fatigues of the first. It is the art of giving pleasure and one must look the part.

A good family: it is a really good thing to be married, to have good children, to be free of the need of being gallant. Ye gods, it is really time one thought about it.

Goodbye. See you soon. Write to me. I shall not leave the country before the middle of January.

Your friend,

DEGAS

4

To Frölich[1]

DE GAS BROTHERS, NEW ORLEANS

27 Nov. 1872

It is only today, November 2nd, that I receive your affectionate letter, my dear Frölich. These most accurate Americans had read Norwick Connecticut where in your handwriting New Orleans was written quite clearly. And so through their fault this good paper has travelled around a fortnight too long.

The ocean! how vast it is and how far I am from you. The *Scotia* in which I travelled is an English boat swift and sure. It brought us (I was with my brother René) in 10 days. The *Empire City* even takes 12 from Liverpool to New York. What a sad crossing. I did not know any English, I hardly know any more, and on English territory, even at sea, there is a coldness and a conventional distrust which you have perhaps already felt.

New York, great town and great port. The townsfolk know the great water. They even say that going to Europe is going to the other side of the water. New people. In America there is far more disregard of the English race than I had supposed.

Four days by train brought us here at last.—Borrow an atlas from your dear little daughter and take a look at the distance. Well (I have certainly not the strength of Thor), I was fatter than on my departure. Air—there is nothing but air.—How many new places I have seen, what plans that put into my head, my dear Fröhlich! Already I am

[1] Lorenz Frölich, Danish painter and designer, who lived in Paris from 1851 to 1872 when he returned to Denmark.

20

giving them up, I want nothing but my own little corner where I shall dig assiduously. Art does not expand, it repeats itself. And, if you want comparisons at all costs, I may tell you that in order to produce good fruit one must line up on an espalier. One remains thus all ones life, arms extended, mouth open, so as to assimilate what is happening, what is around one and alive.

Have you read the *Confessions* by J. Jacques Rousseau? I am sure you have. Then do you recall his manner of describing, his wealth of humour, after he has retired to the île du Lac de St. Pierre in Switzerland (it is towards the end) and that he is telling how he used to go out at daybreak, that whichever way he went, without noticing it, he examined everything, that he started on work that would take 10 years to finish and left it without regret at the end of 10 minutes? Well that is my case, exactly. Everything attracts me here. I look at everything, I shall even describe everything to you accurately when I get back. I like nothing better than the negresses of all shades, holding in their arms little white babies, so white, against white houses with columns of fluted wood and in gardens of orange trees and the ladies in muslin against the fronts of their little houses and the steamboats with two chimneys as tall as factory chimneys and the fruit vendors with their shops full to bursting, and the contrast between the lively hum and bustle of the offices with this immense black animal force, etc. etc. And the pretty women of pure blood and the pretty 25 year olds and the well set up negresses!

In this way I am accumulating plans which would take ten lifetimes to carry out. In six weeks time I shall drop them without regret in order to regain and never more to leave *my home*.

21

My dear friend, thank you a hundred times for your letters and for your friendship. That gives such pleasure when one is so far away.

My eyes are much better. I work little, to be sure, but at difficult things. The family portraits, they have to be done more or less to suit the family taste, by impossible lighting, very much disturbed, with models full of affection but a little *sans-gêne* and taking you far less seriously because you are their nephew or their cousin. I have just messed up a large pastel and am somewhat mortified.—If I have time I intend to bring back some crude little thing of my own but for myself, for my room. It is not good to do Parisian art and Louisianna art indiscriminately, it is liable to turn into the *Monde Illustré*.—And then nothing but a really long stay can reveal the customs of a people, that is to say their charm.—Instantaneousness is photography, nothing more.

Have you seen the Mr. Schumaker whom you sent to me? He thought I should have been able to help him more easily. He wanted to be rubbed down by a French hand, like at the Turkish baths, immediately, after having sweated a little. I told him that it took time to sweat out our vices (well done?).

I shall probably be back in January. I shall travel via Havanna. But you, you will soon be leaving us you say?—I do hope it is for your old mother's sake, in which case it is a duty.—However we shall see a lot of each other until the spring. Your little daughter will play for me—I need music so much.—There is no opera here this winter. Yesterday evening I went to a rather monotonous concert, the first of the year. A Madame Urto played the violin with some talent but rather monotonously accompanied

22

and there is not the same intimacy at a concert, here especially where the applause is even more stupid than elsewhere.

Clotilde must have been delighted to spin you a yarn about the master's journey. I am sure she did not hide her satisfaction. She is a real servant out of a play, but she has her points. I threatened not to take her back on my return and I am afraid to do so. She is too young for a bachelor and her self-assurance is really of too strong a quality. You must still have your Swedish woman, she seems to be so devoted to you that you will not be able to part with her.

You only knew Achille, I believe, and only met him for a moment. My other brother, René, the last of the three boys, was my travelling companion, even my master. I knew neither English nor the art of travelling in America; therefore I obeyed him blindly. What stupidities I should have committed without him! He is married and his wife, our cousin, is blind, poor thing, almost without hope. She has borne him two children, she is going to give him a third whose Godfather I shall be, and as the widow of a young American killed in the war of Secession she already had a little girl of her own who is 9 years old. Achille and René are partners; I am writing to you on their office notepaper. They are earning very nicely and are really in an exceptionally good position for their age. They are much liked and respected here and I am quite proud of them.

Politics! I am trying to follow those of my native France in the Louisianian papers. They talk of little but the super-tax on houses, and they give Mr. Thiers experts' advice on republicanism.

Goodbye, your proverbs are nearly as abundant as those

23

of Sancho; given his gaiety you would increase them three-fold. How healthy a thing is laughter, I laughed at them a lot.

It is true, my dear Frölich, one feels young in spirit. That is what David said in Brussels on the eve of his death. But enthusiasm, good humour and vision, one is bound to lose a little of these. You are in a better way than I am.

You can write to me when you get this; your answer will still find me at Louisiana.—A kiss for your little one. I clasp your hand and thank you for your friendship.

DEGAS

My regards to Manet and his family.

I have reread my letter. It is very cold compared to yours. Do not be angry with me.

5

TO HENRI ROUART

Nlle Orléans, 5 Dec. 1872

You will receive this, my dear Rouart, on New Years Day. You will then wish Mme Rouart a happy New Year and embrace your children for me, including the new born.[1] Out of this you will also take a bit for yourself.

I shall certainly be back in January. To vary my journey I intend going back via Havanna, the French transatlantic lines dock there. I am eager to see you again at my house, to work in contact with you. One does nothing here, it lies in the climate, nothing but cotton, one lives for cotton

[1] Louis Rouart.

24

and from cotton. The light is so strong that I have not yet been able to do anything on the river. My eyes are so greatly in need of care that I scarcely take any risk with them at all. A few family portraits will be the sum total of my efforts, I was unable to avoid that and assuredly would not wish to complain if it were less difficult, if the settings were less insipid and the models less restless. Oh well, it will be a journey I have done and very little else. Manet would see lovely things here, even more than I do. He would not make any more of them. One loves and gives art only to the things to which one is acustomed. New things capture your fancy and bore you by turns. The beautiful, refined Indian women behind their half opened green shutters, and the old women with their big bandanna kerchiefs going to the market can be seen in a different light to Biard.[1] But then what? The orange gardens and the painted houses attract too and the children all dressed in white and all white against black arms, they too attract. But wait! Do you remember in the Confessions, towards the end, Rousseau on the île de St. Pierre on the Lac de Brienne, at last free to dream in peace, observing impartially, beginning work that would take 10 years to finish and abandoning it after 10 minutes without regret? That is exactly how I feel. I see many things here, I admire them. I make a mental note of their appropriation and expression and I shall leave it all without regret. Life is too short and the strength one has only just suffices.— Well then, Long live fine laundering in France.

I have had a slight attack of dyssentry for the last two

[1] The French painter, François Auguste Biard, 1799–1882. He made numerous journeys in the Mediterranean, to Spitzbergen and Brasil.

25

days, and that tires me no end. Nitrate of bismuth will get rid of that. Also, devil take it, we are having temperatures in December which we would be pleased to have in June, 24 or 25 degrees at least, not to mention a sirocco that kills you. Climate that must be unbearable in the summer and is somehow deadening during the other seasons. One has to be of the country or in the everlasting cotton, otherwise beware.

A fortnight ago Mr. Bujac dined at our house. Naturally we talked of you and all the good that was said surprised nobody. He looks very sad and worried, poor man! And he has good cause.—One day I shall go to the glass factory with him.

So you are scarcely more of a writer than I am. Why did you not write a few words yourself? In the morning when the post comes there is very rarely a letter for me and I cannot get used to that.

You see, my dear friend, I dash home and I commence an ordered life, more so than anyone excepting Bouguereau, whose energy and makeup I do not hope to equal.[1] I am thirsting for order.—I do not even regard a good woman as the enemy of this new method of existence.—A few children for me of my own, is that excessive too? No. I am dreaming of something well done, a whole, well organised (style Poussin) and Corot's old age. It is the right moment, just right. If not, the same order of living, but less cheerful, less respectable and filled with regrets.

René is here with his family, he is only slightly homesick. His wife is blind, but she has mastered her mis-

[1] Is this a sincere or an ironical tribute? In any case Degas and his friends used to say of an excessively finished and over 'slick' picture that it was 'Bouguereauté'.

26

fortune. The third child is on the way. I shall be its god-father, but it will not have my obsession. But this is a secret even though the date is the 15th, do not mention it to anyone; we do not speak about it to anyone. I am not even writing about it to my sister. This is an order. Papa wishes the world to end just as if we were not there to make order in it.

The lack of an opera is a real privation. Poor Estelle who is a musician was counting on it. We should have hired a box for her and she would never have missed going except during the actual confinement. Instead we have a company for comedy, drama, vaudevilles, etc. where there are some quite good people and a great deal of Montmartre talent.

The women here are almost all pretty and many have even amidst their charms that touch of ugliness without which, no salvation. But I fear that their heads are as weak as mine, which *à deux* would prove a strange guarantee for a new home. Alas, I have just let out something which is nothing and yet could earn me an atrocious reputation. Beware Rouart, on your honour never to repeat in such a manner that it might be reported to people from here or to people who know people from here that I told you the women of New Orleans were weak minded. This is serious. There is no joking here. My death would not wipe out such an insult and Louisiana must be respected by all her children and I am almost one of them. If in addition I were to tell you that they must also be good, the insult would be complete and by repeating that as well you would have delivered me up once and for all to my executioners. I am exaggerating a little, the Creole women really have something attractive; just now I spoke of

27

Rousseau, I am rereading him in the evenings and I like quoting him.

Julie d'Etange was beloved because she showed herself ready to be loved (reread a letter from Claire to her friend): there is the tenderness of the 18th century in their manner. Of the families here several came over in knee breeches[1] and that flavour has not yet disappeared.

Goodbye, I wanted to fill four pages, be grateful for that, I wished to please you; if I have not succeeded punish me in the same way. And then I am in the office of the De Gas Brothers where it is not too bad for writing. De Gas Brothers are respected here and I am quite tickled to see it. They will make their fortune.

In conclusion I repeat my wishes for a happy New Year to Mme Rouart, I embrace your children once again and clasp your hand.

Your devoted

DEGAS

Greetings to Levert,[2] to your friends, to Martin, to Pissarro with whom I shall have some long talks about here . . . I was forgetting your brother and Mignon.

There is a person here called Lamm who has invented an instrument said to be rather ingenious, which sets buses in motion at the top of the town by means of steam with which it supplies itself. There was a lot of talk about tramways in Paris, I shall bring you a description of this contraption.

---

[1] The costume of the French Noblemen in the 18th century.
[2] Landscape painter who exhibited at the 3rd and 5th exhibitions of the Impressionists. Degas did a portrait of him.

6

To Tissot

DE GAS BROTHERS, NEW ORLEANS

18 Feb. 1873

Tissot, my dear friend, I intended, I was going to reply to your good letter in person. I should have been in London or Paris about the 15 January (such a distance has become immaterial to me, no space must be regarded as great except the ocean). But I remained and shall not leave until the first days of March. Yesterday my trunks and Achilles were ready but there was a hitch which stopped everything. One misses the train here exactly as at Passy. The Saint-Laurent is leaving without us.

After having wasted time in the family trying to do portraits in the worst conditions of day that I have ever found or imagined, I have attached myself to a fairly vigorous picture which is destined for Agnew and which he should place in Manchester: For if a spinner ever wished to find his painter, he really ought to hit on me. *Intérieur d'un bureau d'acheteurs de coton à la Nlle Orléans, Cotton buyers office.*

In it there are about 15 individuals more or less occupied with a table covered with the precious material and two men, one half leaning and the other half sitting on it, the buyer and the broker, are discussing a pattern. A raw picture if there ever was one, and I think from a better hand than many another. (Canvas about 40 it seems to me). I am preparing another less complicated and more spontaneous, better art, where the people are all in summer dress, white walls, a sea of cotton on the tables. If Agnew takes both from me all the better. I do not, however, wish to give up the Paris plan. (This is my present style). In the fortnight that I intend spending here I shall finish the said picture. But it will not be possible for it to leave with me. A canvas scarcely dry, shut up for a long time, away from light and air, you know very well that that would change it to chrome-yellow no. 3. So I shall not be able to bring it to London myself or to have it sent there before about April. Retain the good will of these gentlemen for me until then. In Manchester there is a wealthy spinner, de Cotterel, who has a famous picture gallery. A fellow like that would suit me and would suit Agnew even better. But lets be cautious how we talk about it and not count our chickens too soon.

You are getting on like a house on fire! 900 pounds, but thats a fortune? Ah! if ever! But why not? What a lot of good this absence from Paris has done me in any case, my dear friend. I made the most of it. I have made certain good resolutions which (you will laugh) I honestly feel capable of carrying out. The exhibition at the Academy will have to do without me and I shall mind more than it will. Millais does not understand my little Anglo-American excursion. Anyhow we shall get along all right in spite of that. How much I shall have to tell you about art. If I could have another 20 years time to work I should do things that would endure. Am I to finish like that after racking my brains like one possessed and after having come so close to so many methods of seeing and acting well? No. Remember the art of the Le Nain and all Mediaeval France. Our race will have something simple and bold to offer. The naturalist movement will draw in a manner worthy of the great schools and then its strength

30

will be recognized. This English art that appeals so much to us often seems to be exploiting some trick. We can do better than they and be just as strong.

I really have a lot of stuff in my head; if only there were insurance companies for that as there are for so many things here, there's a bale I should insure at once. This youthful? headpiece of mine is really my greatest asset.

I am very much afraid that Deschamps did not succeed in selling any of my pictures. For the sake of my relationship with Durand-Ruel it is high time that something positive appeared on the debit side of the free-realist stock. From Hirsch I heard that Fantin's picture the *Parnassiens* was sold in London. All the better, he has skill and talent, has Fantin, but too little taste, too little variety, too few ideas. You keep on insisting that over there the place is prepared for a certain number of us. I do believe you, but in my opinion one should go over there oneself to sweep the said place a little and clean it by hand.

What lovely things I could have done, and done rapidly if the bright daylight were less unbearable for me. To go to Louisianna to open ones eyes, I cannot do that. And yet I kept them sufficiently half open to see my fill. The women are pretty and unusually graceful. The black world, I have not the time to explore it; there are some real treasures as regards drawing and colour in these forests of ebony. I shall be very surprised to live among white people only in Paris. And then I love silhouettes so much and these silhouettes walk.

Goodbye, see you soon. The moment I get to Paris I shall write. I intend to take a French boat which docks at Brest. If I take an English one I disembark at Liverpool, in which case I shall see you in London.

31

That fellow Whistler really has something in the sea and water pieces he showed me. But, bless me, there are quite different things to be done!

I feel that I am collecting myself and am glad of it. It took a long time, and if I could have Corot's grand old age. But my vanity is positively American! Good health to you and some 900 pounds more. My brothers are well, their business too. The family has increased by a daughter whose godfather I was. This daughter is, of course, Renés.

I advise you to paint motifs of a varied nature and intensity.

I think we are too fond of the *demi-plein mince*.[1]

I often lecture myself about this and am passing it on to you.

Ever your,

DEGAS

Regards to Millais whom I do not know. Love to Legros, Whistler and to Deschamps if you see him.

Ah! but I nearly forgot something. Go at once to Deschamps. If he still has the *Danseuses* and if Durand-Ruel gives his permission and if there is still time get him to send them to the Paris exhibition, before the 20 March. It is the only picture I could exhibit.

[1] This is an expression coined by Degas and presumably refers to technique. Unlike most of the impressionists Degas laid his colour on very thinly and gave full plastic form to his figures.

32

4. ST. JOHN THE BAPTIST AND YOUTH
BLOWING A TRUMPET

5. SELFPORTRAIT

· 7

TO TISSOT

Paris, Saturday, 1873

MY DEAR TISSOT,

Here I am back again. I shall go and see you soon. We can talk more comfortably.

In the meantime write to me and tell me something about my future with Agnew. Here Durand-Ruel assures me of his devotion and swears he wants everything I do.

But Agnew really intrigues me. I spoke about him casually to a few people and what they told me is absolutely fascinating. They urge me to place myself in his redoubtable hands. Did you tell him the picture I described to you from back there was coming? In a word entertain me with some juicy ideas and some veritable sums of money, for me. I feel absolutely capable of doing my best and of earning an honest living.

How are things with you? At your home they said you were well. I told Sylvain that I should be going to London soon and that if he had something for you he was to give it to me. I hear that you have bought a house. My mouth is still open.

Achille with whom I came back is soon off for Naples.

Look here, Tissot, see that I am more energetic, much more. Back there in an illustrated paper I saw an engraving of a picture of yours, the Thames, with a variation.

I hear you have published an album of children. Tell me where.

I shall pay you a surprise visit very soon and spend 48 hours talking.

33

I did not exhibit. It is better for me to do good work and one fine day to exhibit a whole collection.

My eyes are fairly well but all the same I shall remain in the ranks of the infirm until I pass into the ranks of the blind. It really is bitter, is it not? Sometimes I feel a shiver of horror.

I have too much to say to be able to write.

Goodbye, write soon,

Your friend,

DEGAS

77, rue Blanche.

8

TO TISSOT

1873?

MY DEAR TISSOT,

I should like to spend a few days with you. But I am afraid of missing you, for De Sermet told me that, after the official news he had given you, you were returning.

Returning sounds nice. It is my expression, not his. It would take too long to talk over the whole matter in a letter.

I want to bring several pictures to London. What do you say? We shall have a lengthy conversation after all this time, as they say . . .

This infirmity of sight has hit me hard. My right eye is permanently damaged.

Coloin is a charming man. Give him my friendliest

34

greetings. Durand-Ruel takes everything I do, but scarcely sells anything. Manet, always confident, says that he is keeping us for the *bonne-bouche*.

Goodbye. Write to me. I am curious to hear what you are doing.

Certain parts of my *Orchestre* are done too negligently. At my urgent request Durand-Ruel promised not to send it and he deceived me.

Good night, my dear,

DEGAS

77, rue Blanche.

9

TO HENRI ROUART

Paris, 8 August *1873*

You could not do better, my dear friend, than to sing of the countryside. If your unusual correspondent has not quite burnt down the Opera[1] he has at least rented two rooms ...at Croissy. He is going to go there once he has secured his rest and he will do his nature cure just like any strolling player. He is considering walking to Rouen, along the banks of the Seine, of boarding pinnaces or a train if it happens to pass. So I rather fancy myself a stick in one hand but no parasol, studying values, the curves in the road, on little hills, and above all in the evenings, the hour for soup and of great sleepiness in sheets that are comparatively white. A little whiff of the kitchen and the Roche-Guyon, that is my device. It is *nature*. I am expect-

[1] Allusion to the burning down of the opera rue Peletier in 1873.

35

ing less delirious happiness from it than you, but just a little good for my eyes and a little relaxation for the rest of me.

.   .   .

I have never done with the finishing off of my pictures and pastels etc. . . . How long it is and how my last good years are passing in mediocrity! I often weep over my poor life. Yesterday I went to the funeral of Tillot's[1] father. Lippmann told me the other day that you would soon be back and I had some small hope of seeing you there. I am writing to you in order to reduce the force of your reproaches. Perhaps the letter will come back from Portrieux to Paris but it will reach you and perhaps appease you. The heart is like many an instrument, it must be rubbed up and used a lot so that it keeps bright and well. For my own it is rather you who rub it than its owner.

10

To Faure[2]

Turin, Saturday
Dec. 1873

Dear Mr. Faure,

This is where an ill wind has cast me at Turin. My father was en route for Naples,[3] he fell ill here and left us without any news of himself and when we found him at

[1] Charles Tillot, painter, friend of Degas and of the brothers Rouart. He exhibited with the Impressionists.

[2] The famous singer had been introduced to Degas about 1872 by his friend Manet. See annotations, p. 261.

[3] Laurent-Pierre-Hyacinthe-Auguste De Gas died at Naples on the 23 February 1874.

36

last it was I who had to leave immediately to look after him and I find myself tied for some time to come, far from my painting and my life, in the heart of Piemont.

I was eager to finish your picture and to do your bagatelle. Stevens was waiting for his two pictures. I wrote to him yesterday, I am writing to you today to ask forgiveness from both of you.

Well, here we both are far removed from our own theatres. Even if mine did not burn down it is just as if it had. I act no more.

The papers that I read here speak at great length on the subject of the Opera. There must be some powerful intrigues beneath the surface.

I am not forgetting that I must ask you to give my condolences to Mme Faure. There are some for you too. But all this is very late.

Please accept, dear Mr. Faure, my best regards. And even had these last accidents not occured there would still be excuses.

EDG. DEGAS

Greetings to Lecht.

II

TO BRACQUEMOND

HOTEL DE TURIN
Tuesday, *1874*

A line from Burty,[1] my dear Bracquemond, tells me that yesterday he made a new adherent of you and that you want to arrange a rendez-vous for a talk. To begin with

[1] Philippe Burty, 1830–1890, was one of the first to appreciate and collect original engravings by the great contemporary artists.

37

we are opening on the 15th.[1] So we must hurry. The things have to be handed in by the 6th or 7th or even a little later but in time to have the catalogue ready for the opening. There is plenty of room (*Boulevard des Capucines, former studio Nadar*), and a *unique position etc. etc. etc.* Did Burty give you a little information or would you like to have all the details? I shall give you a date and be prepared to change it if it does not suit you.—*Thursday morning at 11 o'clock at the place itself.*—You will see the premises, we can talk afterwards if necessary. We are getting an excellent recruit in you. Be assured of the pleasure you give and the good you are doing us. (Manet, egged on by Fantin and crazy himself continues to refuse, but nothing seems definite yet from this side.)

Sincerely yours,

DEGAS

77 rue Blanche.

12

TO TISSOT

Friday, *1874*

Look here, my dear Tissot, no hesitations, no escape. You positively must exhibit at the Boulevard. It will do you good, you (for it is a means of showing yourself in Paris from which people said you were running away) and us too. Manet seems determined to keep aloof, he may well regret it. Yesterday I saw the arrangement of the premises, the hangings and the effect in daylight. It is as

---

[1] The first exhibition of painters, sculptors and engravers who were later known as Impressionists. See annotations, p. 261.

38

good as anywhere. And now Henner (elected to the second rank of the jury) wants to exhibit with us. I am getting really worked up and am running the thing with energy and, I think, a certain success. The newspapers are beginning to allow more than just the bare advertisement and though not yet daring to devote a whole column to it, seem anxious to be a little more expansive.

The realist movement no longer needs to fight with the others it already *is*, it *exists*, it must show itself as *something distinct*, there must be a *salon of realists*.

Manet does not understand that. I definitely think he is more vain than intelligent.

So exhibit anything you like. The 6 or 7 is a date but unless I am very much mistaken you will be accepted after then.

So forget the money side for a moment. Exhibit. Be of your country and with your friends.

The affair, I promise you, is progressing better and has a bigger reception than I ever thought possible.

My eyes are very bad. The occulist wanted me to have a fortnight's complete rest. He has allowed me to work just a little until I send in my pictures. I do so with much difficulty and the greatest sadness.

Ever your,

DEGAS

I have not yet written to Legros. Try and see him and stir up his enthusiasm for the matter. We are counting firmly on him. He has only another 60 francs to deposit. The bulk of the money is all but collected.

The general feeling is that it is a good, fair thing, done simply, almost boldly.

39

It is quite possible that we wipe the floor with it as they say. But the beauty of it will be ours.

Hurry up and send.

13

To Bracquemond

Exposition

35, BOULEVARD DES CAPUCINES   *1874*

I should have liked to answer your terrible letter more quickly but I was very hard pressed spending a devilish Sabbath mixed with real summonses. It is on the new paper[1] that I am writing to you in order to soothe you a little and to enable you to laugh at your fright.

You were perfectly right, my dear friend, but with Burty we decided not to let you run away when we had discovered after taking the count that we were nearly all of your opinion and that during the confusion of the first moment only two or three went co-operatively to Charenton.—Factions are rubbish; it is not serious. The fine of 20 francs was a charge that appeared to be something different. Calm yourself completely. It is going very well in spite of so many abstentions.—We are making 200 frcs a day and the advertising was pretty badly done.—On the 1st November we shall be square.

You are very much admired. Those who already knew the drawing saw it again with something more than pleasure not to speak of those who saw it for the first time. So do come here. Burty is upstairs, he never leaves.

[1] Headed: Societé Anonyme Des Artistes, Peintres, Sculpteurs, Graveurs, 9, rue Vincent-Compoint.

See you in a day or two. I am sorry to have been the first cause of your anxiety.

Yours sincerely,

DEGAS

14

TO TISSOT

Paris, Monday

MY DEAR TISSOT,

You recommended these two Americans in rather a vague way. I have only just seen them, a few days ago. One it appears was ill when she got here. And then, too, the time they spent settling down prevented them from showing up sooner. They are not yet sure if they are going to stay in Paris. Who are they? How did you get to know them? Bowles made their acquaintance in the train. There was a brother with them but no one told me anything about him or introduced him to me here. How do they expect to take lessons in comedy and drama when they speak so little French?

How do you expect me to escort them? It is always a question of money and I am not very flush.

You surely promised them much more from me than I can carry out; so you are not doing them a favour.

How is de Nittis getting on over there? Tell me something about it.

My eyes are sometimes quite good, sometimes bad. I am pretty much of a null.

My position in London is in no way assured. Faure will soon be back. His pictures have progressed very little so I should feel rather embarrassed in front of him. There-

41

fore I hardly dare to idle around away from here. I was counting on having something ready for him when I went to London which I should have shown at Deschamps for glory(!) . . . They are not ready.

Ah! if I had my old eyes. But there do not forget me entirely one of these days. Write a little.

Ever your,

DEGAS

15

TO TISSOT

3rd August, Paris.

MY DEAR TISSOT,

In the first place are you in London? I am going to spend two or three days there, no more. As soon as you get my letter send me a wire. Then I could leave to-morrow evening. Alas! I am afraid the Academy will be closed. But all the same we can see your pictures.

Ever your,

DEGAS

16

TO BURTY

1876

Please give me Malassis' no. in the rue Mazarine.

MY DEAR BURTY,

I was still waiting for the proofs from Legros. Be good enough to give them to the Commissionaire. You must have framed some of them. I shall even be delighted if you come this afternoon to dispose of the big passe-partouts that I have.[1]

There are six frames at Durand-Ruels, the two of Malassis and the four large proofs.

There is only just time.

Sincerely yours,

DEGAS

17

TO BRACQUEMOND

Wednesday, 1876

MY DEAR BRACQUEMOND,

Portier[2] whom you asked if there was to be no exhibition,[3] should have written to you at once, as soon as the premises had been found at last, that is to say that the matter was successfully arranged eight days ago. We are opening on the 15th. Everything is being wildly rushed.

You know that the condition imposed, never to have sent anything to the salon, is still in force. You yourself do not, I believe, fulfil this condition, but your wife, is her case the same?

Monet, Renoir, Caillebotte and Sisley did not answer the appeal!

The expenses are covered by means of a combination

[1] This refers to the second exhibition of the Impressionists which took place in April 1876 at Durand-Ruel's, 11, Rue Le Peletier. Degas exhibited *Le Bureau de Cotons à la Nouvelle-Orléans*, today in the Museum at Pau.

[2] Picture dealer and friend of Degas.

[3] The third exhibition of the Impressionists in April 1877.

which I have no time to explain to you. If the entrance money does not cover all these expenses we shall pass a plate round among the exhibitors.

The premises are less big than we need but admirably situated. It is, in a word, the 1st floor of the Dorée house, at the corner of the rue Laffitte.

So please answer me at once and excuse this delay. Portier should have warned you a week ago.

My compliments to Mme Bracquemond.

Your old friend,

DEGAS

19 bis, rue Fontaine.

18

TO FAURE

Friday, *1876*

MY DEAR FAURE,

You said that at the end of this week you would finish paying for the picture even though it is unfinished. It is too early and I am not yet in need of this money.

But if you could let me have another 500 frcs by tomorrow you would give me great pleasure. I shall finish paying everything I had promised to pay by last Saturday.

You are singing tonight, I believe. Do not forget to remind Merante[1] about the photographs he offered me yesterday. I am eager to see them and to work out what I can make of this dancer's talent.

Hoping to see you soon,

E. DEGAS

[1] Dancer, later ballet master at the opera.

44

19

TO FAURE

1876

MY DEAR FAURE,

I am going to return the *Robert le Diable*[1] on Saturday and *Les Courses*[2] on Tuesday.

I had to earn my dog's life in order to devote a little time to you; in spite of my daily fear of your return it was essential to do some small pastels. Forgive me if you still can.

And then, very bad weather for the eyes.

Sincerely yours,

E. DEGAS

20

TO FAURE

March 1877

MY DEAR MR. FAURE,

I received your letter with great sadness. I prefer writing to seeing you.

Your pictures would have been finished a long time ago if I were not forced every day to do something to earn money.

You cannot imagine the burdens of all kinds which overwhelm me.[3]

[1] The *Ballet des Nonnes de Robert le Diable* now in the Ionidès collection in London (South Kensington Museum).

[2] Probably the large *Courses* in the Louvre, Camondo Bequest no. 166.

[3] Degas is doubtless alluding to the trusteeship of his family which he had taken over and which was a burden to him for many years.

45

To-morrow is the 15th. I am going to make a small payment and shall have a short respite until the end of the month.

I shall devote this fortnight almost entirely to you. Please be good enough to wait until then.

Sincerely yours,

DEGAS

21

TO FAURE

Wednesday, 31 Oct. *1877*.
50, rue Lepic.

MY DEAR FAURE,

You will have *Les Courses* on Monday. I have been at it for two days and it is going better than I thought. What is the use of dragging out the chapter of reasons which made me so behindhand? That would do you no good at all.

Sincerely yours,

DEGAS

The *Blanchisseuses* will follow immediately.

22

TO LUDOVIC HALEVY

MENIL HUBERT, PAR GACÉ (ORNE)
Sept. 1877.

MY DEAR HALÉVY,

It seems to me that I told you the other Wednesday that I was going to the country, definitely.

46

Your letter was posted to me by Sabine to the house of the portly Valpinçon where my poor eyes are trying to drink in some green, but it is damp and cold and I am not going to extend my stay until the 15th as I should like to do.

You know, by the way, that I am at your service for Dupuis'[1] studio. It is useless to see bad in it, the thing amuses me very much to do and I shall do it.

So one word and I shall cover the arms of Mlle. Baumaine with a fine washerwoman's lather.

Ever yours,

DEGAS

23

TO BRACQUEMOND

Sunday

I have so little opportunity of seeing you, my dear Bracquemond, that I am all the more sorry to have missed you yesterday. I am rarely at the studio in the afternoon, I go into town almost every day to do a large portrait. Make another attempt in the morning and, if you can, you will give me great pleasure. My best regards to your wife.

Greetings,

DEGAS

[1] This refers to the performances of *la Cigalle*, comedy in 3 acts by Meilhac and Halévy. Dupuis took the part of an impressionist or 'intentionist' painter Marignan. The 3rd act takes place in his studio. Mlle Baumaine played the part of the model Catherine who was posing as a washerwoman. Degas made two sketches of her in one of the albums in which he used to draw in the evenings after dining with Ludovic Halévy.

24

To Bracquemond

Undated

My dear Bracquemond,

Thank you. Go to Gillot without me, I am too busy, I have not the time. Give me the list of what you are sending?—I am trying to make one for myself by repairing old things and building new ones out of them.

Sincerely yours,

Degas

25

To Bracquemond

1879?

My dear Bracquemond,

I shall go and see you one of these days when I have finished two articles[1] which are in the process of making and in the fire.—In the meantime, I should have done better to go and see you a little while ago than to write to you, I am going to ask you if you could employ in the Haviland house a decent man who has been well recommended to me. But he is also a man who from his childhood has been associated with pottery. Would you like me to send him to you? You must not tell him that I delayed at least a week before mentioning him to you.

I have a great need and a great desire to go and talk to

[1] This is the word Degas used for pictures.

48

6. MME JULIE BURTIN

7. MOUNTED JOCKEY

you about the exhibition.[1]—The large composition is superb. What a charming arrangement of types and materials.—I assure both Mme. Bracquemond and yourself that I was fascinated by it.—It is essential to talk about it to say all that one thinks of it.

Sincerely yours,

DEGAS

Wednesday, 50, rue Lepic.

26

TO BRACQUEMOND

Wednesday, 15h.

MY DEAR BRACQUEMOND,

Why did you write to me at such short notice? I arrived as you were leaving, I found your letter at the same time as your card. Why did you not return? You should have realized that however much I did my drawings in town I should be working at the studio even if only for two or three hours a day. And then I lunch every day (with only rare exceptions) at the café de la Rochefoucauld in front of the little market, at the corner of the rue Notre-Dame de Lorette and of the rue Rochefoucauld. That beast of a concierge should really have told you; so it is understood I am there between 12.30 and 1 o'clock.

It is essential to have a talk, there is nothing to equal that. In the meantime for Mme. Bracquemond nothing

[1] Probably the 4th Impressionist exhibition held in April 1879, at 28, avenue de l'Opéra.

49

could be easier. All the cartoons will be placed and well placed. No need for her to worry about that.

So long . . . If I were not afraid of disturbing you or of being unable to talk to you for fear of disturbing your wife I should go to Sèvres one evening, Saturday for example. But I should prefer it if you had time to come here once more.

There is one room with fans, do you hear Mme Bracquemond, up to now, Pissarro, Mlle Morisot and I are depositing things there.

You and your wife should contribute too.

Etc. Etc. Etc.

Hope to see you soon,

DEGAS

The Company Jablockof proposes to do the lighting with electric light. Etc. Etc.

27

TO BRACQUEMOND

13 May 1879

MY DEAR FRIEND,

Yes, certainly, the exhibition[1] has closed. So why do you leave your things? Hurry up. There is also 439.50 frcs to draw per person which is quite good. If you cannot find Portier, our manager, go to 54, rue Lepic where he lives. Or else I shall draw it for you.

I spoke to Caillebotte about the journal.[2] He is willing

[1] The 4th exhibition of the Impressionists.

[2] This journal, called *Le Jour et la Nuit*, never got beyond the project stage.

50

to guarantee for us. Come and talk it over with me. No time to lose!

This morning I went with Prunaire, the wood engraver, you must know him, to see a certain Geoffroy, a famous phototyper, rue Campagne Première.—A strange man, an inventor with bad eyes.

We must be quick and make the most of our gains boldly, boldly above the poor world.

Yesterday a big discussion with Vibert[1] who begs to be told why he is considered stupid.

Congratulations to your wife above all for the two sides of her cartoon.

Yes, indeed, next year we must make a powerful effort. Do find time to spend a day with me. There are a number of things to be fixed and arranged for our journal so that we can show our capitalists some definite programme.

Sincerely yours,

DEGAS

Tuesday 2 o'clock.

28

TO BRACQUEMOND

1879

MY DEAR BRACQUEMOND,

Mr. Ernest May[2] is returning to the attack for your old drawing for which you asked 2,000 francs. He has

[1] Jules Vibert, engraver and painter. He had married Mme Manet's sister, Marthe Leehnoff.

[2] Ernest May, banker and collector with a remarkable flair, friend of Manet. Degas painted his portrait (*A La Bourse*, now in the Louvre). He sold him a watercolour by Bracquemond, *La Lecture de la Bible*, also now in the Louvre.

just offered 1,500. What do you think about it? Let me know. I shall see him in a day or two. He is getting married, is going to take a town house and arrange his little collection as a gallery. He is a jew, he has organized a sale for the benefit of the wife of Monchot, who went mad. You see, he is a man who is throwing himself into the arts. I advise you to accept.

Pissarro has just sent, via the Pontoise carrier, some attempts at soft ground etchings.—How annoying it is that you are so far away . . . when shall we see each other again?

Tell Haviland who was infatuated with a little picture of Mlle. Cassat (sic) and who wished to know the price, that it is a simple matter of 300 frcs, that he should write to me if that does not suit him and to Mlle. Cassat, 6, Boulevard de Clichy if it does.

Pissarro is delightful in his enthusiasm and faith.

Well, Bracquemond, here's to some happy days for us and the feeling of applying a clenched hand to the jaws of our best artists.

Sincerely yours,

DEGAS

Your four frames are at my house, they were lying around for anyone to take. The cartoons alone, because of their size, were in no danger. You can take your engravings away after we have talked about the journal.

29

TO CHARLES EPHRUSSI[1]

Undated

I should have liked to meet you the other day at your home or yesterday at the Opera. Can you come, don't dress at all, a frock-coat will do, on Thursday evening punctually at 9 o'clock, 21 rue Pigalle, 3rd floor. Just a little house warming. We shall be very few, but merry.

Greetings,
DEGAS

30

TO BRACQUEMOND

*End of 1879 or
beginning of 1880*

MY DEAR BRACQUEMOND,

I have seen May. The matter is settled. But I think, and I told him so, that it will be necessary to have another frame. As a result of all the removals your drawing went through with me, the frame finally fell to pieces. What do you want to do?

The grains[2] are progressing satisfactorily, even without you (who should by rights be teaching us instead of leaving us to find our own way.)

Greetings,
DEGAS

[1] Director-owner of the *Gazette des Beaux Arts*, who owned some very fine works of Degas.

[2] Aquatint grains on copper. B. was an expert in this material. Degas refers here to the plate he was preparing himself and to one Pissarro was engraving.

53

To Bracquemond

1879–1880

How I need to see you, Bracquemond, and how badly I let you down!

1st. Let me know if my friend Rossana[1] could work in your Haviland house; he is a man of much talent, landscapist and animal painter, very sensitive, should be able to do flowers delightfully, grasses etc. I was supposed to have written to you about him a long time ago.

2nd. We must discuss the journal. Pissarro and I together made various attempts of which one by Pissarro is a success. At the moment Mlle Cassatt is full of it. Impossible for me, with my living to earn, to devote myself entirely to it as yet. So let us arrange to spend a whole day together, either here or at your house.—Have you a press at your place? Your wife is still preparing her exhibition, is she not?

See you soon,

Degas

I heard that you have the commission for Delacroix's Boissy d'Anglas.[2] It is what you so much wanted. Long live the leading profession!

---

[1] Degas seems to have been very fond of Rossana; he dedicated one of his finest monotypes to him (*Femme dans son bain*).

[2] The beautiful engraving after Delacroix's *Boissy d'Anglas* in the museum of Bordeaux is one of Bracquemond's masterpieces.

To Bracquemond

1879–1880

The Salmon[1] is annoyed and wants all the plates by Tuesday. A word to the wise is enough. I am working at my plate,[2] strong at the great game.

Could you come and bring me your plate on Tuesday morning or else go straight to Salmon and give it direct for press? It is too bad that you cannot come about 5 o'clock. The whole bunch of us will be there.

Greetings,

Degas

Sunday morning.

33

To Bracquemond

1880

My dear Bracquemond,

It is opening on April 1st. The posters will be up to-morrow or Monday. They are in bright red letters on a green ground. There was a big fight with Caillebotte as to whether or not to put the names. I had to give in and let him put them up. When on earth will they stop the headlines? Mlle Cassatt and Mme Morisot did not insist on being on the posters. It was done the same way

[1] Famous printer of engravings. His firm still exists.
[2] Refers to the well-known plate *Au Louvre, Musée des Antiques.* See pl. 18 and 19.

as last year and Mme Bracquemond's name will not appear—it is idiotic. All the good reasons and the good taste in the world can achieve nothing against the inertia of the others and the obstinacy of Caillebotte.

In view of the frenzied advertisement made by de Nittis[1] and Monet (in the Vie Moderne) our exhibition[2] promises to be quite inglorious. Next year I promise you, I shall take steps to see that this does not continue. I am miserable about it, humiliated.

Start bringing your things. There will probably be two panel screens, one in the centre of the room with the four windows and the other in the entrance room. You will be able to arrange your entire stock of engravings on them.

See you soon,

DEGAS

If you insist and Mme. Bracquemond insists too her name can be put on the second thousand posters during the exhibition. Answer.

34

TO CAMILLE PISSARRO

1880

MY DEAR PISSARRO,[3]

I compliment you on your enthusiasm; I hurried to Mademoiselle Cassatt with your parcel. She congratulates you as I do in this matter.

[1] Joseph de Nittis, 1845–1884, painter and engraver.
[2] The 5th exhibition of the Impressionists, held in April 1880.
[3] For the relationship between Degas and Pissarro see Pissarro's letters to his son Lucien, ed. Rewald, Kegan Paul, London 1943.

Here are the proofs: The prevailing blackish or rather greyish shade comes from the zinc which is greasy in itself and retains the printers black. The plate is not smooth enough. I feel sure that you have not the same facilities at Pontoise as at the rue de la Huchette.[1] In spite of that you must have something a bit more polished.

In any case you can see what possibilities there are in the method. It is necessary for you to practise dusting the particles in order, for instance, to obtain a sky of a uniform grey, smooth and fine. That is very difficult, if one is to believe Maître Bracquemond. It is, perhaps, fairly easy if one wants only to do engravings after original art.

This is the method. Take a very smooth plate (it is essential, you understand). Degrease it thoroughly with whitening. Previously you will have prepared a solution of resin in very concentrated alcohol. This liquid, poured after the manner of photographers when they pour collodion onto their glass plates (take care, as they do, to drain the plate well by inclining it[2]) this liquid then evaporates and leaves the plate covered with a coating, more or less thick, of small particles of resin. In allowing it to bite you obtain a network of lines, deeper or less deep, according as to whether you allowed it to bite more or less. To obtain equal hues this is necessary; to get less regular effects you can obtain them with a stump or with your finger or any other pressure on the paper which covers the soft ground.

Your soft ground seems to me to be a little too greasy. You have added a little too much grease or tallow.

[1] At the planisher Godard.
[2] A small sketch of a plate, held by a hand, with drops trickling off it is attached.

What did you blacken your ground with to get that bistre tone behind the drawing? It is very pretty.

Try something a little larger with a better plate.

With regard to the colour I shall have your next lot printed with a coloured ink.[1] I have also other ideas for coloured plates.

So do also try something a little more finished. It would be delightful to see the outlines of the cabbages very well defined.[2] Remember that you must make your début with one or two very, very beautiful plates of your own work.

I am also going to get down to it in a day or two.

Caillebotte, so I am told, is doing the *refuges of the Boulevard Haussmann* seen from his window.

Could you find someone at Pontoise who could cut on very light copper some things traced by you? That kind of pattern could be applied on a line proof—touched up a little for effect—of etchings or soft ground etchings and then the exposed parts printed with porous wood coated with water colours. That would enable one to try some attractive experiments with original prints and curious colours. Work a little on that if you can.—I shall soon send you some of my own attempts along these lines.[3]— It would be economical and new. And would I think be suitable enough for a beginning.

No need to compliment you on the quality of the art of your vegetable gardens.

[1] Pissarro had no press of his own and during his brief visits to Paris used to get proofs pulled either by Salmon or Delatre or Degas.

[2] Pissarro had done a soft ground etching of a cabbage field (Delteil, no. 23).

[3] As far as we know Degas never carried out these attempts. The process of coating with water colour was first used by Gauguin, on wood, which he had engraved himself.

58

Only as soon as you feel a little more accustomed try on a larger scale with more finished things.

Be of good cheer,

DEGAS

35

TO CAMILLE PISSARRO

1880

MY DEAR PISSARRO,

Here are two postcards which were sent to me from Cadarts. What does it mean? Answer Marchand yourself.

Mlle Cassatt is trying her hand at engravings, they are charming. Try and come back soon. I am beginning to advertise the journal[1] on various sides. With our deliveries of proofs *avant la lettre* we shall cover our expenses. That is what several collectors of engravings have told me.

Greetings,

DEGAS

36

TO EUGÈNE MANET

Undated

MY DEAR MANET,

I went to see your premises in the Chaussée D'Antin. They seem to me to be very difficult to exploit

[1] Le Jour et la Nuit.

59

for us. The garden would be an excellent place but it cannot be unplanted. The first room, the court with the windows is also quite good, but the remainder are dark. I sent Rouart to see the premises and we have not yet been able to discuss them.

On the other hand there is the *Café du Grand Balcon* on the *Boulevard* in the same block as the *Opéra Comique*, which seems to me to combine all the advantages: eight good rooms and others. Steps leading to the Boulevard itself. Portier is thrilled with it and so am I. Do go and see it. The only difficulty is the question of covering the walls, which are decorated and must be treated with care, with a wooden screen. That might be rather expensive.

A thousand things to your terrible wife.[1]

Sincerely yours,

DEGAS

Tuesday morning.

37

TO MADAME DIETZ MONNIN

Undated

DEAR MADAME,

Let us leave the portrait alone, I beg of you.[2] I was so surprised by your letter suggesting that I reduce it to a boa and a hat that I shall not answer you. I thought that

[1] Berthe Morisot.

[2] The portrait in question is an oil painting of Mme Dietz-Monnin which, we believe, Degas destroyed. He kept some very advanced studies. One of these in pastel and turpentine shows the lady in a pink hat with a large boa round her neck (1st Vente Degas, no. 116 and 2nd Vente Rouart, no. 77).

60

Auguste[1] or Mr. Groult[2] to whom I had already spoken about your last idea and my own disinclination to follow it, would have informed you about the matter.

Must I tell you that I regret having started something in my own manner only to find myself transforming it completely into yours? That would not be too polite and yet...

But, dear Madame, I cannot go into this more fully without showing you only too clearly that I am very much hurt.

Outside of my unfortunate art please accept all my regards.[3]

38

TO CAZIN

29 Oct. *1880*

MY DEAR CAZIN,

Here is the Duranty[4] sale approaching. It must be made to be a little productive. Could you give something? Let me know.—I am going to Legros and Fantin.—You know that this sale is the sole resource of the old woman. —It will take place in about a month's time.

Sincerest greetings,

DEGAS

19 bis rue Fontaine.

[1] Auguste de Clermont, son-in-law of Mme Dietz-Monnin, a friend of Degas.

[2] Manufacturer of Italian paste products and a famous collector of eighteenth century work.

[3] This letter was found among Degas' papers, unsigned.

[4] The sale after the death of Emile-Edmond Duranty held in January 1881 at the Hôtel Drouot. See annotations, p. 262.

39

TO CAZIN

29 Nov. *1880*

MY DEAR CAZIN,

Mr. de Liesville is urging me to call everyone together for the Duranty sale. You have promised to give me something. I am even forced to be indiscreet. Will Mme Cazin also be kind enough to give something?— Let me know at once (the catalogue is about to be made). Just give the title or titles, you can send the things later. I am also writing to Fantin. Could you write to Lhermitte who like you must be in the country.—I have delayed, it is my fault, try and help me to make it good. You must also begin a campaign to have your 'articles' pushed by amateurs, admirers of yours.

Yours in haste,

DEGAS

40A

TO HENRI ROUART

Paris, Tuesday 26 Oct.

Thank you for your pencilled letter, my dear Rouart. The sirocco, it appears, dries up the ink as it does oil colours and the vitality of the painters. Ah! how I regret not having been able to go down there with you to see these dear friends. And then, to tell you at once, it is comparatively rare, I am in the mood to love grand nature a little. You would have had as companion a changed

62

being and one strong enough to vibrate like anyone else. The result might have been some fine drawings or pastels done by a frenzied Grevin[1] beside himself. And the sublime would doubtless have been just as good for me as for any sage.

We can hardly see at all here. The afternoons in particular it is night. I should like to finish Ephrussi's picture and even though the canvas and the drawings are up to date it is scarcely progressing at all. And yet there is some good money at the end of it, which is eagerly awaited.

Bring me back some fine outline drawings as you can do them. Did you take pastel with you? Water colour is thin[2] . . . and yet Delacroix!

At Burty's there is a tiger by him in pastel which under glass looks like a water colour. It is pastel put on very lightly on a slightly glossed paper. It is very vibrant, it is a lovely method.

I am going to write to Cherfils,[3] I neglect him too much. And yet one does not often meet such affectionate and intelligent beings as he is.

The Cassatts have returned from Marly. Mlle. Cassatt is settling in a ground floor studio which does not seem too healthy to me. What she did in the country looks very well in the studio light. It is much stronger and nobler than what she had last year. I shall be seeing you soon, with your articles before us in the rue Lisbonne we can talk more freely. I am writing for fear of your malediction.

[1] Alfred Grevin, founder of the waxwork show in Paris. See annotations, p. 263.

[2] Degas very rarely used aquarelle or even wash.

[3] Alphonse Cherfils, friend of Degas and of Paul Lafond (see Lafond, Degas, vol. II, frontispiece).

63

I am just off to the Boulevard Voltaire to dine with your brother. Mud, mud, mud, umbrellas. In the evening hours it is nevertheless very beautiful!

40B

To Christian Cherfils[1]

I am expecting you, we shall talk of poetry, that's a promise, whenever you like. I am reading the Traité de Poesie by Banville. I have bought a copy of Ronsard and even a bad tool, a dictionary of rhymes. Enclosed: Petite Danseuse.[2]

See you soon,

Degas

41

To Alexis Rouart

1882

My dear friend, it was only yesterday that I had this little attempt with carbon crayon printed.[3] You see what a pretty grey it is. One should have emery pencils.[4] Do give me an idea how to make them myself. I could not talk about it with your brother on Friday. Thank you for the stone you gave me. It scratches copper in a most delightful manner. Is it a conglomorate like Denis Poulot

[1] Poet, son of Alphonse Cherfils.
[2] See annotations, p. 263.
[3] See annotations, p. 264.
[4] A conglomoration of emery dust.

64

8. MME HERTEL

9. WOMAN WITH CHRYSANTHEMUMS. MME HERTE

makes? With the magnifying glass I read Delanoue the Elder.

On what could I use it as an etching point?

No time to do some really serious experiments. Always articles to fabricate. The last is a monochrome fan for Mr. Beugniet.[1] I think only of engraving and do none.

Greetings,

DEGAS

42

TO HENRI ROUART

2 May *1882*

Lafond sends me a few words. He is going to come here to see his charcoal drawing at the salon only to return immediately to his lyceum at Pau. The fine weather is coming to us and doubtless to you too? Sunday great varnishing day. An astonishing Whistler, excessively subtle but of a quality! Chavannes, noble, a bit of a rehash, has the bad taste to show himself perfectly dressed and proud, in a large portrait of himself, done by Bonnat, with a fat dedication on the sand where he and a massive table, with a glass of water are posing (style Goncourt). Manet, stupid and fine, knows a trick or two without impression, deceptive Spanish, painter . . . in a word you will see.[2] Poor Bartholomé is ruffled and is asking naïvly to have his two things back.

[1] Picture dealer in the rue Laffitte.
[2] The picture referred to is the *Bar aux Folies Bergères*.

65

43

To Albert Hecht[1]

Undated

My dear Hecht,

Have you the *power* to get the Opera to give me a pass for the day of the *dance examination*, which, so I have been told, is to be on Thursday?

I have done so many of these dance examinations without having seen them that I am a little ashamed of it.

Warmest greetings,

Degas

Tuesday morning.   19 bis, rue Fontaine St-Georges.

44

To Albert Hecht

Undated

My dear Hecht,

I am still convinced that I put my address without my name. You were very kind to look everywhere for me. But what ceremony!

I thought I could slide into the Opera amongst the others with a slip of paper and you want to lead me in person to the feet of Mr. Vaucorbeil.[2] Till Tuesday then, with excessive thanks.

E. Degas

Sunday morning.

[1] Albert Hecht, a collector, friend of Manet and Degas. In Degas' picture *Robert le Diable* he is represented looking through his opera glasses from the orchestra stalls.

[2] Director of the Opera from 1879-1884.

66

45

To Henri Rouart

De Pau, *Undated*

My dear Rouart,

I am writing to you from Lafond's room, rue du Lycée at Pau. I had word Sunday morning from Christian Cherfils, informing me in the briefest and saddest way that his father, desparately ill, had ordered him to send his farwell greetings to me. That moved me so much that I took the evening train to get here on Monday.

Cherfils had been very bad, he is better and those around him think that he is out of danger. So I am leaving tomorrow or the next day. As soon as I am in Paris I shall give you full details.

From what I heard your wife say on Friday you were at the Queue on Sunday. And so I did not go to you before leaving.

Warmest greetings,

Degas

(A postscript by Lafond follows on the same page.)

46

To a Friend

Undated

Dear Sir,

I saw you at the circus a few days ago. Perhaps you are still in Paris so this little roll which contains the

67

carricature of me by Pellegrini,[1] found at last, may have some prospect of reaching you. I had given up all hope of being able to return it to you, it was stuffed away where, by rights, I ought never to have found it. In a word here is your little treasure.

Lepic,[2] too, is hard to find. Is he at Berck, or at Tunis or in Italy? I do not know myself but they tell me that he is definitely separated. Have you like myself retained some pleasant memories of the times spent with this queer fish? Have you still the intention of coming to say how do you do to me *en passant?*—19 bis rue Fontaine St. Georges.

Please accept my warmest thanks.

DEGAS

Tuesday morning.

47

TO J. E. BLANCHE

1882

DEAR MONSIEUR BLANCHE,

I shall enquire at the Opera if they have a seat free for the three days. I shall take Monday as I always have done and you will make arrangements with a friend for the other two days, like you told me. The seat will be in my name and I shall have the right to go behind the scenes.—This is a first suggestion which I consider much

[1] A painter and friend of Degas. In the Tate Gallery is a portrait of him painted by Degas.

[2] Count Lepic, painter and engraver, who taught Degas the art of making monotypes. He was also a great dog breeder. See annotations, p. 265.

too agreeable for me and not enough so for you. Going behind the scenes attracts you and I am preventing it. But perhaps you are the kind of man either to console yourself, or as art critic to have permission in any case or simply as a spoilt child to demand it as a right.

Vaucorbeil is still ill and Ephrussi (Charles) on the best of terms with Darcel, the secretary of the Opera.

On the other hand I do not know if it will be easy to find someone to replace me for Monday's seat in which case I shall be saddled with it until a new subscriber takes it off me. And then your letter makes me think that you thought I had a subscription for all three days and was willing to give up two, more particularly one day. No, I only have Mondays and that is sometimes too much.

And then I should like to keep the right side. Tell me if you have a friend all ready to take the third day. This is all rather difficult to arrange.

With regard to the sending of the huge sum, we are still far removed from that.

Write to Ephrussi, he will dictate your, he will dictate our, conduct.

Sincerest regards,

DEGAS

48

To J. E. BLANCHE

July 1882

Thank you, dear Monsieur Blanche, for the parcel; I was helped with the translation of this difficult piece.

69

I am writing to you from Halévy's house, at Étretat, where the weather is fine, but more Monet than my eyes can stand.

Greetings,

DEGAS

49

TO BARTHOLOMÉ

Paris, 5 August 1882

I have surprised you my dear friend. It is true I am down and up again very quickly. And so I arrived Monday evening, I found your message and the next morning, Tuesday, rue Bayard, they told me that you had already decamped the evening before. Eight days at Etretat, it was a long time for me. Halévy[1] is good but mournful, I can neither play piquet nor billiards nor do I know how to pay attentions to people nor how to work after nature nor simply how to be agreeable in society. I think I weighed a bit heavily on them and that they had thought I was more resourceful.

When are you coming back? For I am alone here. Paris is charming and is not work the only possession one can always have at will?

Monday morning sitting with Pagans,[2] before his de-

[1] At this time Halévy had suffered several bereavements as the result of which he gave up writing for the theatre.

[2] Spanish singer and guitarist, much admired by Degas' father. Degas painted several portraits of him, playing the guitar with the father listening (one is in the Louvre, another one, exhibited Gallery Petit 1924 no. 8, was sold for 85.000 fr. at the sale H. Fèvre in 1925).

70

parture for Spain. Mme Camus[1] is said to have wept for spite and for passion for the guitar in front of a good general who teaches her.

J. E. Blanche sent me a big article in the Standard where I was flattered in a few courteous and pinched lines. I should pinch them too were I not afraid of spoiling the abscess before it is ripe. He is said to have tried to get hold of Gervex again, a new man decorated and more useful.

.   .   .

50

To Bartholomé

HOTEL BEAUSÉJOUR
Veyrier, 9 Sept. 1882

Not to finish at the Salon, a life spent elsewhere—in the kitchen.

These are the worst moments when one must use one's brains.

De la Croix has the name of a painter.
To fire without seeing, that is love itself.
Chance has come down to earth and they say she flies.
They have stolen her ugliness from her.
There are travellers more fortunate than I am.
Do I travel myself, said a station master?

---

[1] Mme Camus, the wife of a friend of Degas. He painted a magnificent portrait of her sitting at a piano (1st Vente Degas, no. 111). There were many pencil and pastel studies for this portrait at the sale of Degas' Studio.

51

To Heymann

On a visiting card, undated

My dear Monsieur Heymann, come to-morrow to see how your drawing is framed. I think the edge must be left white. Moreover, you will see. Do not come after dark.

Greetings,
Degas

Saturday night.

52

To Heymann

Undated

Dear Monsieur Heymann,

Let me go once more with the Italian and French dancers for lunch on Sunday at Boldinis. But for Sunday week let us swear on our lives, both of us, that we shall have neither dancers nor funerals nor anything whatever on that final day.

A thousand apologies,
Degas

Friday.

53

To Bartholomé

Wednesday, *Spring 1883*

Change of air, that must do you good even in this filthy weather! That must cure you of not being warmed all day by a stove, warmed also by painting. I really must force myself, now that the days are growing longer, only to

72

remain half the day, either morning or afternoon, in my studio, and to go for walks. *Ambulare*, here is a new motto, *postea laborare*.[1]

Manet is done for.[2] That doctor Hureau de Villeneuve is said to have poisoned him with too much diseased rye seed. Some papers, they say, have already taken care to announce his approaching end to him. His family will I hope have read them before he did. He is not in the least aware of his dangerous condition and he has a gangrenous foot.

54

To Henri Rouart

16 Oct. *1883*

My dear friend, this letter will just reach you at Venice. So the separation that Mme Rouart wished for will be less complete than necessary.

On Saturday we buried Alfred Niaudet.[3] Do you remember the guitar soirée at the house, nearly a year and a half ago? I was counting up the friends present, we were 27. Now four have gone. The Mlles Cassatt were to have come, one of them is dead. That would have made it five. Let us try and stick to this earth however republican it may be.

.   .   .

You love nature as much as humidity. In spite of that

[1] From this time on Degas was obsessed by the idea of these walks which later became a veritable ambulomania. At the end of his life he used to spend hours wandering round Paris; he was then almost blind and in permanent danger of being run over.

[2] Manet died in spring 1883.

[3] Alfred Niaudet, a cousin of Mme Ludovic Halévy, died in October 1883. Degas painted a portrait of him (Degas' exhibition, 1924, no. 61).

73

do me the favour of leaving your two friends for a moment to go, in dryness, to the palais Labia to see, partly for yourself and partly for me, the frescoes of Tiepolo. Forain, yes Forain, gave me a glimpse of them on the table at the Café La Rochefoucauld, which he terminated by comparing them to a poster by Chéret. It is his way of admiring them. Perhaps it is no worse than any other.

.   .   .

Had I accompanied you I should have given a prelude to the portrait of your daughter, in the heart of Venice, where her hair and her complexion were once famous. But I remained here because there are such things as rents.

55

To Ludovic Halévy

Nov. 1883

My dear Halévy,

You must know what a dancer is like who wants you to put in a word for her.[1] She comes back twice a day to know if one has seen, if one has written.

Are you better? If you have the courage or the strength write a line to Vaucorbeil, to Mérante, not about her engagements which would be silly, but about her dancing and her past and her future.

I had no idea what such an enthusiast was like. And she wants it done at once. And she would like, if she could, to take you in her arms wrapped in a blanket and carry you to the Opera!

Greetings,

Degas

[1] Mlle Chabot, dancer at the opera.

74

To Ludovic Halévy

Nov. 1883

The little Chabot arrived both very surprised and very pleased at having been called to M. Meyers to renew her engagement. The Mlles Salle[1] and Sacré were called at the same time.—She was offered a sum that she says is very small. She was getting 2.200, they offer her 2.400. We must try and help her to get 2.600 or 2.800 for the first year. Moreover Mr. Meyer offers her 2.700 for the next year, that is to say for 1885; and for 1886 3.000 francs. So it is an increase of 200 francs or 300 francs at most for which she is asking for this year and she says that she deserves it for all sorts of reasons: she was a pupil at 16 years, she was moved up after each examination etc. . . .

So try to get her:
1st. 2.700 francs or 2.800 francs for 1884;
2nd. 3.000 francs for 1885;
3rd. 3.500 francs for 1886.
The contract she has to sign is for 3 years.

The petitioner is in a great hurry and quite simply wishes you to go to the Opera this evening. I am much afraid that you will have to go to the *Rois en Exil*[2] or even to *Simon Boccanegra*[3] where I am presenting myself this evening at no. 177 in the name of Mr. Verdi.

In a word, do what you think best, write to Mr.

[1] Mlle Salle, dancer at the opera. Degas did a beautiful pastel portrait of her in 1886, three views of her head on the same sheet (Degas' exhibition, 1924, no. 159).
[2] A play by Alphonse Daudet.   [3] Opera by Verdi.

Vaucorbeil, for it would seem to be really urgent. Moreover you know how everything is done at the Opera.

Greetings,

DEGAS

The said demoiselle Chabot sends you her respects.

57

TO HENRI LEROLLE

4 Dec. 1883

My dear Lerolle, go at once to hear Thérésa at the Alcazar, rue du Faubourg-Poissonnière.

It is near the conservatoire and it is better. It has already been said, a long time ago—I do not know what man of taste said it—that she should be put on to Gluck. At the moment you are all absorbed in Gluck. It is the right moment[1] to go and hear this admirable artist.

She opens her large mouth and there emerges the most roughly, the most delicately, the most spiritually tender voice imaginable. And the soul, and the good taste, where could one find better? It is admirable.

See you on Thursday in any case at *my* musician.

Greetings,

DEGAS

[1] Recitals of *Orpheus* were given at the house of the composer Ernest Chausson, brother-in-law of Henri Lerolle. Degas enjoyed them very much.

76

58

To M. and Mme Bartholomé

Undated

Monsier Degas, much touched, presents his compliments for the New Year to Monsieur and Madame Bartholomé. He also finds himself forced to admit that he has no visiting cards and that when he does not find people at home he writes his name on the margin of the concierges' newspapers; he is given an envelope. The delicacy and finesses of friendship in others gives him infinite pleasure. May the others continue!

59

To Madame de Fleury[1]

8 Jan. 1884
21, rue Pigalle

. . .

On Saturday, at the Studio, the first sitting took place for an intimate portrait in which Mr and Mme Bartholomé are represented in their town attire.[2] Their departure for the country did not exhaust my good will and in a week I shall be ready for them if they are for me.

Whose turn? Yours, dear Madame, and your very excellent husbands, but come back!

Your old friend,

Degas

[1] Mme Fleury, sister-in-law of the sculptor Bartholomé.
[2] We know nothing of the existence of such a portrait.

77

60

To Madame de Fleury

Monday

Just imagine I have an engagement for Saturday and am heartbroken. Really I am being pampered and the time will come when I shall pay for that with ruin. In the meantime I shall dance no more, or rather make others dance no more; for some considerable time there have been no more little dears at my house. I really must return to it seeing that, as you say, it is wisdom I need above all things.

A thousand apologies,

DEGAS

61

To Madame Bartholomé
(née de Fleury)[1]

Undated

DEAR MADAME,

Be good enough to grant me yet another little leave of absence for Wednesday. Something surprising has happened. A painter Henri Lerolle[2] who, so I was told, was in the process of being decorated in the space left empty between his Salon and the Exposition Triennale or Nationale and whom I knew to be quite well off,

[1] First wife of Bartholomé.
[2] See the article by Maurice Denis, *Revue de Paris* 10 Nov. 1930.

78

has just invited me to dinner. The right he has is still recent, but fairly weighty. In agreement with his wife, who is said to manage him, he has just, at a moment like this, bought a little picture of mine of horses, belonging to Durand-Ruel.[1] And he writes admiringly of it to me (style Saint-Simon), wishes to entertain me with his friends and although most of the legs of the horses in his fine picture (mine) are rather badly placed, yet, in my modesty, I should very much enjoy a little esteem at dinner. Just this once, dear Madame, permit me to become intoxicated with the perfume of glory, from the other side of the water, behind the Invalides, Avenue Duquesne. If nothing happens to intoxicate me, not even the wine, why should I not go and present myself to you for a moment, about 10.30, with an air of success.

Your friend,

DEGAS

Monday.

62

TO BARTHOLOMÉ

16 Aug. *1884*

So you are going to proceed by way of confiscation, my dear friend? What will you confiscate in the horrible human heart? I do not know where my friends can sit down in it, there are no more chairs; there is the bed which cannot be confiscated and where I really sleep too

---

[1] This picture was bought by Lerolle from Durand-Ruel in 1884 for the comparatively high sum of 3.000 francs (Lafond, Degas, vol. II and Degas' exhibition, 1924, no. 45).

79

much, for this morning at 7 o'clock, after having left it for a moment to go and open the window and set about writing to you before the postman left, I remained there in order to enjoy the morning more deeply. Yes, I am getting ungrateful, and I am getting so in a state of coma, which makes this illness irremediable. After having cut art in two, as you remind me, I shall cut my own beautiful head in two, and Sabine[1] will preserve it for its shape's sake in a jar.

Is it the country, is it the weight of my fifty years that makes me as heavy and as disgusted as I am? They think I am jolly because I smile stupidly, in a resigned way. I am reading Don Quichotte. Ah! happy man and what a beautiful death.

Let your wife, being in such good health, not curse me too much and let her ask herself if I am really worth the trouble. And let her keep her anger and her tenderness for a man who is young, confident, proud, simple, bold and soft, supple and hard, painter and writer, writer and father, and even more astonishing than he thinks, writes or lets others write and says so: Long live J. F. Raffaëlli. He is, I tell you, the man we need.

Your medallion should have angered me. And I cheered it as if it were of gold. Long live Sandoval too, the man who lets houses, the man who pays his rent, without in any other way judging of your merit.

I am cracking coarse jests for you and I have not the taste for them. Ah! where are the times when I thought myself strong. When I was full of logic, full of plans. I am sliding rapidly down the slope and rolling I know not

[1] Sabine Neyt, one of Degas' maids who died at his home in the rue Pigalle.

80

where, wrapped in many bad pastels, as if they were packing paper.

Goodbye, my sincere regards all the same to your excellent wife and to you.

DEGAS

63

TO HENRY LEROLLE

21 Aug. 1884

If you reply, my dear Lerolle, you will most certainly tell me that I am a queer specimen. Why did I not write to you, before your departure, and after having received the box of sugared almonds,[1] really I hardly know. If you were single, 50 years of age (for the last month) you would know similar moments when a door shuts inside one and not only on one's friends. One suppresses everything around one and once all alone one finally kills oneself, out of disgust. I have made too many plans, here I am blocked, impotent. And then I have lost the thread of things. I thought there would always be enough time. Whatever I was doing, whatever I was prevented from doing, in the midst of all my enemies and in spite of my infirmity of sight, I never despaired of getting down to it some day.

I stored up all my plans in a cupboard and always carried the key on me. I have lost that key. In a word I am incapable of throwing off the state of coma into which I have fallen. I shall keep busy, as people say who do nothing, and that is all.

[1] It is customary in France for parents to send boxes of sugared almonds to their friends for the baptism of their children. The box in question was for one of Lerolle's sons.

81

I write you all this without real need to do so, it would have sufficed to ask your pardon very humbly for my rudeness.

But I remember that Alexis Rouart told me that on leaving Paris you were going near Vimoutiers. This letter that I am addressing 20, Avenue Duquesne will follow you and this time (it is you who must answer me) I am sure of a reply.

I must tell you that I, too, am near Vimoutiers with a friend[1] of my childhood days, perhaps only a few leagues from you. Write to me to Château de Ménil Hubert, par Gacé (Orne).

If you are where I think you are I shall go and see you at once.

My kind regards to your wife.

Sincerely yours,

D.

64

TO DURAND-RUEL

Paris 1884–85

DEAR MONSIEUR DURAND-RUEL,

For want of big money send me small, by Prosper,[2] to-morrow Thursday. Damnable life. I am finishing your devilish pictures.

[1] Paul Valpinçon, son of Edouard Valpinçon, the friend of Ingres. He was the father of Hortense Valpinçon. He and Degas had studied together and all his life he remained one of Degas' most devoted friends. Degas painted several portraits of him (one of them now in the Coll. Marcel Guérin).

[2] Prosper Garny, an employee of Durand-Ruels. He attended to all Degas' numerous removals and installations.

82

M. Casburn was to have come today to bring the picture of the orchestra. He did not come.

Greetings,

DEGAS

65

TO LUDOVIC HALÉVY

MÉNIL HUBERT, PAR GACÉ (ORNE)
1884

You saw how de Nittis died, how quickly one dies! I managed to arrive in time for the funeral. There is nothing one can say to his wife.[1] She is with the Groults at Vitry. I have news of her from Mr. Groult. As soon as I get back to Paris I shall go and see her. She loved her husband well, but she fussed over him too much. We shall have a talk about this unhappy woman and this strange and intelligent friend.

66

TO HENRI ROUART

CHÂTEAU DE MÉNIL HURERT, GACÉ (ORNE)
22 Aug. *1884*

My dear friend, the other day Mme Rouart's letter was brought to me in the cab which was taking me to Normandy, your concierge will have confirmed this.

[1] Degas did a portrait of Mme de Nittis in a wicker chair (formerly Coll. Manzi).

83

I should have been pleased to see you and had I known you were arriving at 5 o'clock on Friday the 9th I should have gone straight away in the evening to the rue Lisbonne. I kept on postponing and postponing. My aunt had a rather disgruntled, rather imperious letter written to me. Whereupon I announced that I would be there at the said time.

And now the weather is magnificent, weather *for you* (at bottom I am not really wicked), but I have no real confidence in the aneroïd barometer which says that it is to continue. One should believe in nothing but rain, in France. Here we are in a hollow. Large park, very high dense trees and water which rises everywhere from under your feet. There are some pastures where it is like walking on sponges. Why do the animals that feed and do their business in these damp pasturing grounds not get rheumatism and why do they not pass it on to us who eat them?

I am trying a little to work. The first days I felt stifled and dazed by the amount of air. I am recovering, I am trying to eat little. Well, however do you manage to arrive in a country, quite unprepared and work the next day at 6 o'clock in the morning, the same day if you travel at night? You love nature more than I do, you will reply. Meanwhile it is I, not you who am face to face with nature. And in spite of all I am a little beside myself. I am attempting work which would take 10 years to finish and I leave it after 10 minutes without regrets, said Rousseau in the île de St.-Pierre.

Well it is a long time since we saw each other, my dear friend. My absence has been enormous, it will soon be over. I cannot say quite definitely if I am not very well here.

I can feel that your wife is angry with me, that I have

84

10. SELFPORTRAIT

11. EDOUARD MANET

not behaved well to you, that I arranged my departure badly to coincide with your arrival. It is true. I shall do better another time.

As I shall still be facing nature for another short week and as I did not reply to your good letter from Mans, I am counting on a word from you, who are never angry with me. Your daughter, who already had such a pretty complexion before, must be quite dazzling now, she should come out.

A thousand greetings,

DEGAS

67

To GEOFFROY
At the Court of Justice, rue Faub. Montmartre, 10 or 12

Undated

DEAR MONSIEUR GEOFFROY,

Be good enough to tell me if your terrible patron[1] is here. The other day at Raffaëllis we decided to have a little soirée at the Opera, a soirée of connoisseurs. I am writing to you as if he were not here. It is a little as if I were writing to him himself and he turned out to be here. The soirée will be to-morrow, *Faust*. Reply by carrier.

The man of Asnières[2] has written something about Honfleur which I liked very much and which almost made up for the fat volume he had dedicated to his exhibition and to HIMSELF.

Kind regards,

DEGAS

Tuesday 4 o'clock. 19 bis, rue Fontaine.

If Clemenceau is here and if he is not free to-morrow

[1] Clemenceau.   [2] Rafaëlli.

and he prefers Friday to Wednesday tell him there is the *Africaine* on Friday, but it is an ultimatum and I am going to the country on Saturday for a fortnight.

68

To Ludovic Halévy

Ménil Hubert 1884

MY DEAR HALÉVY,

I am here in Normandy for another 10 days. Will there still be time on my return, to go and see the very pleasant house at the seaside? Keep Cavé there, who is also most agreeable. I myself will be as agreeable as I know how. Moreover I am getting more so according to what they say here.

Kind regards to Louise[1] and to the man of taste,[2] if he is still there.

Sincerely yours,

DEGAS

69

To Ludovic Halévy

Ménil Hubert 1884

MY DEAR FRIEND,

Sabine quite simply posted on your telegram which reached me this morning Saturday, which, apart from its urgent friendliness, is not otherwise serious.

[1] Mme Ludovic Halévy.

[2] Albert Cavé, son of Mme Elisabeth Boulanger-Cavé, the friend of Delacroix. (Ingres painted her beautiful profile!) There is a pastel portrait by Degas of Cavé and L. Halévy behind the scenery of a theatre (Degas' exhibition, 1924, no. 140).

86

But! this bust![1] so you think it is nothing, you do not believe that *I am fanatically keen about it with* (style Goncourt) *a family bending over my talent?* You want me to take advantage of the fine weather and leave, and they put it forward to make me stay. And then there is the bust, I swear to you that it is a bust with arms and that I want to press on with it. If I leave it, it is lost.

Look here, by arriving towards the end of next week, one could still be well received if you are still there, could one not?

But I shall miss Cavé, that is the meaning of your wire.

Best regards to Louise and to you,

DEGAS

To come straight to Dieppe from here without passing through Paris. I leave that problem to your great mind.

70

TO A POET
(STEPHANE MALLARMÉ?)

Undated

DEAR SIR,

I took two days to write to you in prose and you two in verse. Had I felt like spending a whole winter in peace I should have liked to attempt the sonnet of the dog,

[1] Degas had undertaken to do a bust of Hortense Valpinçon. It was one of the first of Degas' sculptures though he had already exhibited the wax statuette of the little dancer of 14 years at the 5th impressionist exhibition. Unfortunately this bust was broken whilst it was being cast. Degas preserved the back for some time in his studio, but in the end it melted. See p. 91, 1.

87

of the little dog who plays the trumpet with its tail. I should certainly have spent the whole winter on it and touching it up would have carried me over into the spring. I admire you, you can play with such burdens and take your time over them. Thank you very much, but I shall not conceal from you that you humiliate me with pleasure.

Your very humble servant,

DEGAS

Monday.

71

TO HENRI ROUART

Saturday

My dear friend, I, too, go to the country. But what terribly fine weather, what heat and how badly I can stand it! As I should sleep all day and as I am writing to you about 4 o'clock with the shutters closed, it will not last or else I shall return to town, where the too beautiful weather is yet easier to bear.

Le Mans is 20 leagues from here, doubtless you are still there, but I have only just arrived, and it must keep for another time. And then this evening a family is arriving who would not like to be the pretext for my flight.

Your good letter nearly missed me. I begin by placing all my sentiments at the feet of your terrible wife, whom I never visited and who finds it so hard to forgive people who are not as good as her husband who, so she says incessantly, is too much so. I am not well versed in arguments to appease her and I prefer repeating all manner of

88

compliments on the young aquarellist to whom she gave birth...

... What you tell me about young Colin makes me very eager to see his sketches. How lovely natural dispositions and talent are—and how necessary it is to have something more!

I am anxious to rest and to regain the taste for work. In spite of the difficulties of the situation I had been sunk in gloom. It will be terribly necessary to stop up the gaps. I have made a few sales which will secure me until the end of this year. So all is not disheartening.

72

To Henri Rouart

MÉNIL HUBERT, PAR GACÉ (ORNE)
Undated

I shall return to Paris all the same, my dear friend, bursting with health and after one of the longest stays in the country that I can remember.

The reason is a large bust with arms which I have undertaken of young Hortense and which I am finishing very patiently and very laboriously. The whole family and their friends are here to supervise me and I must confess, a horrible doubt seems about to vanish from their pleasant faces. How I floundered at first, ye Gods! And how little we understand what we are doing if we do not let our craft take a little care of the things that we need. It is all very well to say that everything can be done by simplicity; one does perhaps succeed, but how disgustingly.

89

And then with this damned bust I am neglecting my business. I should have been in Paris some time ago, to do at least what I *have to do*. And what I *have to have* is not going well either. It will be necessary to deal with it.

Until next week, I cannot overstay it without being doomed to ruin and perhaps infamy. All my kind remembrances to the vindictive Mme Rouart and to the young florist whose simple and attractive talent I have not, I swear it, concealed here. There are two persons here, Hortense and Mlle Pothau who talk marriage from morning to night. It is incredible what must be going on inside these heads.

Sincerely yours,

DEGAS

73

TO LUDOVIC HALÉVY

Ménil Hubert

MY DEAR FRIEND,

I am very much afraid I shall not get there at all. I am being kept or rather I alone am keeping myself here until the end of the week to finish a bust with arms. It is long but most amusing. And the interest shown me resembles malignant curiosity. Which results in a fanatic effort on my part to obtain a likeness and even something more.

Once in Paris my first task will be to finish a commission. But will there still be time to go to Dieppe? Do not be angry with me and expect me all the same, one fine day

90

when it is fine. I see that you are even more satisfied with the man of taste. And I shall miss him!

My regards to Louise.

Sincerely yours,

DEGAS

Ménil Hubert, par Gacé (Orne).

74

TO BARTHOLOMÉ

MÉNIL HUBERT
Monday, *15 Sept. 1884*

The little ointment, made by your own hands, my dear friend, reached me—I rubbed it on and cannot deny that it did me good. One can return from further afield.

If you wish me to tell you why I am still here I shall do so —'So you are doing nothing of Hortense[1], said her mother to me? Then who do you imagine will do anything?' And so as to occupy myself I set to work on a large bust with arms, out of clay mixed with small pebbles. The family follows my work with more curiosity than emotion. In a word one only amuses oneself with things one cannot do if one is as ill-balanced as I am. And except for my legs which are boring into my body and my arms which by dint of stretching are tiring my stomach, things are not too bad. I shall certainly be back in Paris by the end of this week, and after a few weeks spent in earning my bread it will be necessary to return to Normandy with a moulder to assure

[1] Hortense Valpinçon, later Mme Jacques Fourchy. Degas painted her portrait in oils when she was a child (Exhibition, 1924, no. 33). One drawing of her, as a young girl (in profile), is in the possession of her heir; another one, touched up with pastel, in the Coll. M. Guérin.

91

the cast and also the durability of the work. The family will and is assisting as Norman peasants, doubt painted on their faces and installed deep in their hearts.

75

To Bartholomé

MÉNIL HUBERT
Friday, *3 Oct. 1884*

I cannot resist the vanity of the poet, my dear friend, and the madrigal I am sending you, which according to custom has been done *negligently* and with the inconvenience of an after thought, will give you an idea of my way of being gallant and idiotic. A comedy for four people entitled *Le Rival au Berceau* was acted a few days ago for the first time and yesterday for the second time by Mlles Valpinçon and Pothau, Mrs. Felotrappe and Louis Brinquant (the first a Desgenais, a Landrol, the second a young leading comedian, a Coquelin). I took no part in the play and to hide my mortification whilst exploiting it, I wrote in blank verse the small piece that follows: it was but little understood, it was too subtle, but an odour of old world gallantry was discovered in it which, you know well, has always been personal to me. Here it is:

You wished to give pleasure
To Yourself
By acting in a play
And it is us that you delight!
If you did not get full measure
Of what you desired to-night,
To applaud we alone have the right.

92

The public acclaims from all sides:
All! All!
Ah! Youth so gay
The ear hears less than beholds the eye
And I dare swear that is why
One must laugh today
That you, traitress fair,
Should be in despair
At being better than the play.

The reference at the end seems to me to have been noticed; I emphasized it enough I can assure you, and in this light and appropriate vein, it is in good taste.

I can feel the collar of my blue suit with the gold buttons rising to the nape of my neck and . . . stroking it, for it is in this suit that you will have the goodness, one of these days, provided you are here in time, to beg them to bury me. In growing old everything transports me to the rococo of 60 years ago. It is there that Raffaelli d'Asnières sees me and you too perhaps, man of taste.

With regard to the bust, let it suffice you to know that it is not finished, that it is horribly long, that I am returning to Paris on Sunday to finish some things and secure the inviolable rent for the 15 of this month. There are two arms, I have already told you so; let it suffice you to know as well that naturally one of them, where the hand is visible, is behind the back. Also I am perhaps the only one for whom this goes very well.

Write to me to Paris. Good health, particularly for your wife who deserves it more than you do. Also greetings.

DEGAS

93

76

To Durand-Ruel[1]

MÉNIL HUBERT
Summer 1884

DEAR SIR,

My maid will go and fetch a little money from you. She sent me this morning a threat of seizure from the taxes. I had payed more than half. It appears that the state wants the remainder immediately.—Fifty francs will suffice. But if you could give her a hundred she could keep something for herself. I left her with very little and I am prolonging my stay here a little where it is so beautiful. Ah well! I shall stuff you with my products this winter and you for your part will stuff me with money.

It is much too irritating and humiliating to run after every five franc piece as I do.

Warmest greetings,

DEGAS

Château de Ménil Hubert, près Gacé (Orne) Wednesday.

77

To Durand-Ruel

Dieppe, Oct. 1884

DEAR MONSIEUR DURAND-RUEL,

I received your mandate safely. If you could send me another for 50 francs I should be provided for. I

[1] Durand-Ruel were Degas' bankers. They advanced him money and he paid with his pictures, for which they had the monopoly.

reckon to be back on Wednesday during the evening. Enough of idling.

You are quite right. What lovely country. Every day we go for walks in the surroundings, which will finish up by turning me into a landscapist. But my unfortunate eyes would reject such a transformation.

I sympathize deeply with you in your Paris prison. And yet you will see with what serenity I shall return.

Kind regards,

DEGAS

Saturday. Still with Halévy, rue de la Grève, Dieppe.

78

TO HENRI ROUART

Monday morning

MY DEAR FRIEND,

I know quite well that you are returning soon and that I could easily not write to you. And then I have so little to tell you. As a matter of fact though, one often writes to one's friends to tell them nothing and that nevertheless implies that one was so pleased to receive something from them, to know that they are thinking of one and to be their friend.

So in the first place give my regards to Mme Rouart. The waters did her good last year. Very likely she is better because of them this year. That is already something.

X... must have rejoined you. This guide of the Pyrenees gave me the impression the other day of being very downhearted. We had met in the neighbourhood of the Goupil house and he seemed fairly resigned to see the money coffers of this great house closed to him for ever. He would have thought, or have had me believe, that Cabanel had something to do with it, had I not told him that that was another illusion and that it all came from higher up and much further away.

I am joking, my dear friend, for want of something better to do. And how can one listen seriously to the misfortunes of others when one considers oneself so much above them in that respect. Really it is too much, so many necessary things are lacking at the same time. In the first place my sight (health is the first of the worldly goods) is not behaving properly. Do you remember saying one day, we were speaking of someone I cannot remember whom, who was growing old, that he could *no longer connect*, term applied in medicine to impotent brains. This word, I always remember it, my sight no longer connects, or it is so difficult that one is often tempted to give it up and to go to sleep for ever. It is also true that the weather is so variable; the moment it is dry I see better, considerably better, even though it takes some time to get accustomed to the strong light which hurts me in spite of my smoked glasses, but as soon as the dampness returns I am like today, my sight burnt from yesterday and broken up today. Will this ever end and in what way?

79

TO PORTIER

Undated

MY DEAR PORTIER,

Will you come and fetch your pastel on Sunday morning?

At Mr. Coedis, 8 rue Bayard, a friend and neighbour of the Bartholomés, there is a small Corot for sale, authentic and with a known history. I saw it yesterday and I was told that the owner would be very willing to give it up. Raffaëlli was to speak to you about it himself. In any case I am writing to you. Go there, and first of all, knock at the Bartholomé's door which is opposite.

So until Saturday,

Regards,

DEGAS

Thursday.

80

TO HENRI ROUART

Undated

I am going to be punished, my dear Rouart, my letter will catch up with you in Paris, already back from Argelès. However what calms me a little is a letter from Cherfils this morning who speaks of you as if you were still his neighbour (or nearly so) and he should be well posted.

So Cauterets, according to the papers, is the centre of

97

elegance in the Pyrenees and from what you tell me I see that Argelès is no less well provided for.

Go to, search no more for a site in the wilderness! Every year you have the same regrets and it is only right. The fortifications here are visited by more simple folk, certainly more to your taste, and you flee them. If it were not for the sake of joining your family I could not understand your going so far. Long live the suburbs. I continually revert to this because I feel that there in my hand lies the key to a great truth and this hand is not quite closed.

Cherfils writes from St.-Jean-de-Luz. Will you go and see him? (It is possible that you have already seen him on your way back from Paris and that this letter is de trop.)

When you are back for good you must come to the house at Louveciennes and you will tell me all the news. The acqueducts of Louis XIV are there, Monsieur Rouart, and they are good and the Marly watering place too. And one thinks of Madame Dubarry who would not have had her head cut off had she loved her pavilion less, her sweetmeats and her diamonds shut up in a chest of Sèvres china. There you are!

81

To Madame Ludovic Halévy

Friday

My dear Louise,

I am asking for leave of absence for to-morrow. I intended going in person to beg you for it and I did not do so. And Reyer? How eager I am to hear his

98

arrangement. He must on no account forget me for the rehearsal.[1]

One does not know how to keep fit in this awful weather. It is useless for the models to tell me that the others are in just as bad form as I am, I cannot reconcile myself to doing so little and so badly.

I send you as well as the academician my warmest greetings.

DEGAS

82

TO BARTHOLOMÉ

Friday, *19 Dec. 1884*

I was waiting for news from him instead of going right ahead. It is because, at bottom, I have not got much heart. And what I once had has not been increased by the sorrows of my family and others; I have been left only with what could not be removed, comparatively little, which is sufficient for myself but which is not sufficient for my good friends.

You two have always been so full of goodness and tenderness towards me. You are both, the one in illness, the other in the pain of incertitude and I chose this moment for not returning to you what you gave to me. Thus acts a man who wishes to end his days and die all alone without any happiness whatever.

[1] A rehearsal for Reyer's opera *Sigurd*.

99

83

TO HENRI ROUART

Wednesday, *1884 or 1885*

You are coming back, my dear Rouart, and I could quite well not answer you, but in a little while the redoubtable Mme Rouart will say to me: 'Have you written to Henri?'

It is not possible that over there you are not enjoying the same fine weather that we are having here, and that the aquarelle is not progressing.

I can see X . . . weighing you down. Heavier than air, Bouguereau, you will see, will yet end up by lifting him into his nacelle like Rousselin. We are friends without ballast and without weight. We shall remain on earth and shall know how to console ourselves.

I am just off to the portrait exhibition. I have been deeply engrossed and deeply irritated by the need for fabrication. Oh Ye Gods.

Very little time spent on the portrait of your daughter in spite of the pleasure it gives me to do. Oh Ye Gods!

Come back. I do not like writing.

84

TO MME HENRI ROUART

Tuesday evening, *1884 or 1885*

DEAR MADAME,

Here is your excellent husband giving me the slip for Thursday. To-morrow, Wednesday, I was to have gone to your house, a little for his sake. For I want to put

12. SELFPORTRAIT   D.L.

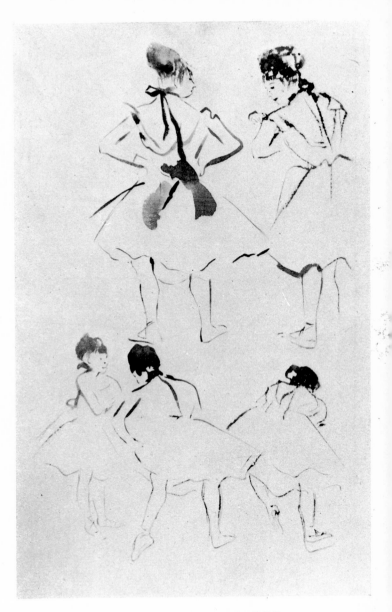

13. BALLET DANCERS

him in your place in the portrait and it would have been a good thing for me to make a little preliminary drawing of him in proportion to his daughter. So please give me leave of absence and believe in my unbearable friendship.

DEGAS

85

TO BARTHOLOMÉ

1 Jan. 1885

My dear friend, the apples are better than you think and than they look. So much for the mouth.—With reference to the heart I should very much like to see you again both of you. So come back. One will be better to you than one has ever been.—The coming year will see me good.

So come back, my dear friend. My most affectionate wishes.

DEGAS

86

TO DURAND RUEL

Paramé, *Aug. 1885*

MY DEAR MONSIEUR DURAND-RUEL,

I shall not return to Paris until Saturday. 'One' is going to Mont-Saint-Michel till Thursday, I should like you to send me a little supply of money in an ordinary envelope, not registered. I am afraid of being short when it comes to settling up. Address it Grand Hotel Paramé, par Saint Malo.

101

With regard to the simple white frame which is to replace the one of the horses, oblong size, there are several of both sizes at my place 21, rue Pigalle. Sabine will show them to you. Send Prosper with the measurements, he could even take the frame from the horses that are in my room.

Hoping to see you soon,

DEGAS

87

TO DURAND-RUEL

Paris, *Dec. 1885?*

MY DEAR DURAND-RUEL,

Here I am again asking you for money. Can you send me another 500 fr. this morning or this afternoon (after 2 o'clock)?

In the meantime here are some sketches. Haviland[1] came yesterday to buy something from me and he seems to have decided on one of the broad pictures, which, fortunately, is the furthest advanced. He wanted to buy it from me. I had to send him to you. It has been arranged that you will write to him the moment you receive the thing.

Happy New Year. Yesterday I should have gone to the rue de la Paix if I had been able to leave the vicinity of a small place to which nature kept sending me.

Sincerely yours,

DEGAS

[1] Charles Haviland, manufacturer of Limoges china, for whom Bracquemond had done a lot of work. Cf. Venturi, Archives II, 102.

102

88

To Durand-Ruel

Paris, *1885?*

My dear Monsieur Durand-Ruel,

To-morrow, Saturday, I should be much obliged if you could send me a little money. I can scarcely continue to draw from little Closet in the rue de la Chateaudun. I have already delivered several drawings to him and I must wait until he sells them.

The frame for the *Harlequin*[1] is at my house. I could give it to Prosper or Henri if you send one or the other to me.

Greetings,

Degas

89

To Ludovic Halévy

Wednesday, *Aug. 1885*

My dear Friend,

I just learnt from her own lips of the departure of our beautiful friend.[2] But grief was immediately followed by a desire to laugh at your farewell preparations made so

---

[1] Degas did several pastels of a harlequin with dancers (see Lafond, vol. II). This harlequin must have been one of the girl dancers (Mlles Saulaville and Alice Biot) who played the parts of the two harlequins in the ballet *les Jumeaux de Bergame* by Florian (music by Lajarte, ballet master, Mérante). Degas had assisted at the rehearsals in 1885.

[2] Mme Howland, friend of Fromentin. The letters of which his book, *Maîtres d'Autrefois*, is composed, were originally written to her. She was going to America.

103

far in advance. So it is still the man who rises at 5 o'clock so as to leave at 8 o'clock; the academy has not turned him against the railway guide. Look here, if you are going to meddle with it, shall we see any clearer? and more quickly.

So our beautiful friend is coldly sad and I can guarantee that the three men who will be at Le Havre to the minute at the appointed hour will have difficulty in not shedding a tear. But that must not be arranged in advance.

Go, hang yourself. One has found, without effort, a better combination than yours. You know that I am just returning from a delicious tour and that after Mademoiselle Alice Piot,[1] the Mont St. Michel and the inn of Madame Poulard made the most impression on me. Well, nothing would appear simpler to you than our plan. The day is not yet fixed and, being what we are, cannot be until the last moment. But this is the itinerary. The company is Mme Howland, Cavé and I. The luggage for the journey is sent direct to Havre. Then we go to Michel, we stay there a few days. The date, the 29th by the way, is the only one fixed. Thence we reach Caen where the little boat, which never travels without warning you, will bring us to Havre. There is still one doubtful point, Cavé, the man of taste, who might have the idea not to be one of us.

Go to then, work out this new itinerary seeing that you are a member of the Academy.

Greetings to Louise. I embrace your son.

Sincerely yours,

DEGAS

[1] Dancer at the opera.

104

90

To Cavé

Ah Cavé all our life, Mme Howland and I, we suffer from your incertitude. I am writing to Reyer. I think he will come. There will be spiced veal as well. And you, ye gods, will you come?

Greetings,

Degas

91

To Alexis Rouart

Monday, *1885*

My dear friend,

I am very much afraid I shall not be one of you to-morrow. General rehearsal of Sigurd[1] very probably. And it is essential to go with the friends of Reyer, Halévy, Cavé. It is an event. All the same I am very sorry to abandon you.

Sincerely yours,

Degas

92

To Ludovic Halévy

Sept. 1885

My dear friend,

I have forgotten to write down Mme Howland's address, send it to me. Tell Cavé that I should be much

[1] First performed in Paris on June 12, 1885.

105

obliged if he would go and buy me the chestnut handkerchief with the blue border, that that damned shopkeeper near the Place Duquesne will not part with for less than 5 francs. This damn handkerchief must be in my house.

Very difficult to resume the honourable habits of the studio; had I stayed any longer the thing would have become difficult, really.

Greetings to everybody. Ask Daniel to tell our dear little companions that I miss our happy walks very much.

Sincerely yours,

DEGAS

Saturday.

Watch over Barnes[1] whilst protecting him so that he may quite simply be happy.

Sir Rivers Wilson,[2] it seems to me, deserves an apotheosis.

93
TO BARTHOLOMÉ

Undated

He is here, I looked at him again this morning, with the *folds of his buttocks over his red loins.* Goncourt thinks and writes in this manner when his friend Bartholomé sends him a pumpkin.

We shall eat it for supper on Sunday, my dear friend. I and some persons who admire the opera and who under-

[1] Photographer at Dieppe. Degas and his friends had found him living in great want at Dieppe. They had given him work all through the summer.

[2] Financier, a friend of Edward VII, then Prince of Wales.

106

stand food. I shall try not to eat more than they do, even less.

But when are you coming back? I ask you that and I forget that you love the fields, that you are an amateur of gardens and that it is there that I shall go one day to place a Wagnerian slab above your head. So I am the bear, lightly ruling modern sculpture, more habitually sucking the honey of the Hymettus in the Opera *Sigurd*. I saw it again, this *Sigurd*, and just missed seeing Reyer again at the Brasserie Müller, to the right of the monument.— Divine Mme Caron,[1] I compared her, speaking to her in person, with the figures of Puvis de Chavannes which were unknown to her. Rhythm, rhythm, may your excellent wife give it back to me one of these days in front of infamous Reyer, the master of his score!

The pumpkin was delicately outlined, was it not? Ah! if one could only draw a noble fountain like that with rounded shoulders. For lack of grown ups who do not want to let themselves be seen (Sabine) there are children built like that.

I wrote a note to your sister-in-law. Give her my kindest regards once more. Sincere greetings to both of you. You could write to me apart from vegetables, it would give me great pleasure too.

Sincerely yours,

DEGAS

Wednesday: Any news?

---

[1] Famous singer, created Sigurd and Salammbo. Her greatest roles were Elisabeth in *Tannhauser*, Elsa in *Lohengrin*, Iphigenia in *Iphigenia in Tauris*. Degas wrote a sonnet dedicated *à Mme Rose Caron*.

107

94

TO LUDOVIC HALÉVY

Tuesday, *Sept. 1885*

Here in three envelopes, my dear friend, are the photographs for the young and beautiful Sickert.[1] To avoid going to the post office I invented this method without difficulty.—That does not prevent Whistler from stunning one. What do I hear? That you are going to write an analysis of the lecture, translated by Louise, in the Hébrard of the *Temps*? If it is done seriously I shall laugh academically. If you are introducing the 'Ten O'clock' then it is irony, it is contempt of the arts by the people of the world in full dress, it is happiness. The man in the cap[2] leaves you the choice between the two styles—what does he want; for himself, it is quite simple.—He wants you to talk about him after him.

Yesterday the man of taste at Sigurd. He is to deliver a fresh lot of groups to me. Normandy handkerchiefs cost 15 francs at Rouen. We made them rise in price. The pelisses are going to be at top prices. I have stood firm until now and have not given mine. But for my promise to Louise I really think I should have been despoiled.

This morning your Blanche sends me his group with Dinah,[3] accompanied by a charming message. He is reserving me a Dinah alone. He has resumed his sittings with

[1] At that time Sickert was living near Dieppe.

[2] Whistler. He had given a lecture to a circle of friends in Dieppe at which several French and English artists and writers had assisted. These included George Moore, the Cobdens, Lady Archibald Campbell, Helleu.

[3] Housemaid of Mme Blanche's mother, who acted as a model.

the little Carracciolo.[1] And I envy him. What a change for me, what a pleasure it would be for me to draw such grace.

The arms of Mme Caron are still there. How well she is able to raise her thin and divine arms, holding them aloft for a long time, without affectation, for a long time and then lowering them gently! If you see them again you will cry out: Rachel, Rachel, just as I do, whose taste you despise as well as the deep understanding of the human heart and the human body.—That is all.

On the whole Barnes is scarcely unhappy any more.

Are my dear little companions well? Give them my most affectionate greetings, also to the Sickerts. Come back. Your sons are growing into very charming boys. I look at their portrait, at the one of their mother and at the one of their father with a sort of affection. My regards to everyone too, including Mme Ingres.[2]

GERMAIN[3]

95
TO LUDOVIC HALÉVY

Wednesday, *Sept. 1885*

The silver frame delicately chased was a bargain. You did not know that, nor that the object cost only 1.100 francs, because it was a bargain. Does she know it, she Madame Mérante?[4] Moreover, were she to know it she would say: it is a bargain, it is true, it cost less, but after

[1] Mlle Olga Carraciolo, daughter of the duchess of Carraciolo.
[2] This was Degas' name for Mme Blanche.
[3] One of Degas' christian names: Edgar, Germain, Hilaire.
[4] Mme Mérante, ballet instructress at the opera.

109

all, me, I am gaining by the bargain! You wrote thus in the days when, without being an academician, you thought and wrote like Madame Cardinal!

Thank you very much, my dear friend, for the proofs that Cavé brought me! When you have others I shall receive them with pleasure. Have you managed to compose for Barnes an apotheosis on Rivers Wilson with Duchess,[1] and several Polonaises? I know that 11 of the Blerzy servants were to have posed. Gervex also told me, told us (for Cavé was there one evening of Sigurd) about the departure of Dr. Blanche with the duchess; the scene of the duchess in English, the English translated for you by the painter Jacques,[2] Mme Blanche at the door of the carriage, more preoccupied with her husband's gallantries than with her sensible son, indignant at this supervision etc . . ., etc.

It would have been better to have grouped my three muses and my two choir children against a white or light background. The attires of the ladies in particular are lost. It would also have been better to compress the people more.[3]

My regards to everyone. What lovely weather today, for Arques, for Varengeville with my dear walking companions. Cavé brought some touching messages from them. And the Sickerts.

October is approaching and we shall see each other again a little.

Greetings,

DEGAS

[1] Duchess Carraciolo.　　　[2] Jacques-Emil Blanche.
[3] Refers to an apotheosis composed by Degas as a parody on Ingres' Apotheosis of Homer.

96

TO BERTRAND[1]

5 Jan. 1886

SIR,

I had heard in Paris of your nomination and it is in Naples where I have been for several days that I have the pleasure of reading it in good print.

Both you and Monsieur Gailhard[2] have been so charming to me, you have favoured me so exceptionally, that I feel myself a little attached to your fortunes and that I am getting to be, as they say, one of the household. And I have seen in this house so much activity and lavishness expended in spite of all conceivable difficulties, that in wishing you a Happy New Year, benefits and good health included, I am merely doing my duty. The title Chevalier will also suit you very well, Monsieur, and I shall hasten to the Opera as soon as I return to shake hands with you very respectfully.

Please give Monsieur Gailhard all my best wishes and friendly regards.

E. DEGAS

Naples[3]

---

[1] With Colonne co-director of the opera.
[2] Since 1884 art director and from 1893–1907 director of the opera.
[3] This letter, stained with ink, was found amongst Degas' papers.

III

To Bartholomé

Naples, 7 Jan. 1886

Dear and Excellent friend, I found your letter very much in evidence on my dressing table when I reached Naples. Thank you very much. Your heart is full of goodness towards me, and you are always careful to let me know it quickly. I wish I were already back. Here I am nothing more than an embarrassing Frenchman. The family is going away. All the world, almost, is divided. May they soon return me to my palace of flames like the Valkyrie, that is to say to my studio heated by a good stove. Hagen[1] is acknowledged here.

Happy New Year to your wife and to you. I have just forced myself to write and even when writing to you I get no ideas. I shall write you a long letter another time. And do you know what I am going to do before dinner, to rest and get a little air? No, you do not know that I am going to walk down as far as the Palais Gravino, that is to say the post, to expedite four letters of four pages each—then in a tram reach Pausilippe via Ste Luce as if it were the Trocadero.

Warmest greetings,

DEGAS

My sister[2] and Lucie[3] send their thanks. Write again.

Calata Trinita Maggiore, Napoli.

[1] Figure from *Sigurd*.
[2] Thérèse De Gas, wife of Edmond Morbilli.
[3] Lucie De Gas, first cousin of Edgar. She was the daughter of his father's brother. Her daughter, Mme Boffi, still inhabits the Palazzo de Gas in Naples, Calata Trinita Maggiore.

98

To Ludovic Halévy

Naples, 7 Jan. 1886

My dear Halévy,

Had you not been elected member of the Academie Francaise you would not have had to devote a whole term to writing the speech you will have the pleasure of reading during my absence to a select audience, and (I am sure, I don't know why, of what I am putting forward) you would be in Naples with me, preferably at Rebouleau; at Naples, for my benefit, you would have unfolded all the qualities of the lawyer which all the world recognizes in you. And you yourself, such a good judge of everything that is not art,[1] you recognize it first of all. Can you picture me, without you, deprived of that polished lucidity of yours, conversing in Italian with the ancient advocate (lawyer here is advocate) of my unhappy family! This man, really a man of confidence, explained everything to me with such perfect simplicity that I understood absolutely nothing but what I already knew. The presence of an academician, as well versed as himself on all kinds of subjects, would have struck him very forcibly. And during all that time I should have served as an unintelligent interpreter, which is my real profession in this country.

I am in joint-tenancy with my cousin Lucie, a minor and very nearly of age. Both of us are interested in breaking it up. She because she is of an age to get married and her fortune might suffer from my continued presence here;

[1] Whenever the subject of painting came up in a conversation with Degas, Halévy was in the habit of listening and of declaring his incompetence.

113

I because it is my wish to leave behind the name of a good painter in France rather than of a small landowner in Italy, whilst all the same obtaining a small sum of money. So I have to see that my share is purchased at as high a price as possible. You would be wonderful in an affair of this kind. Write to me at once, between two visits to Doucet,[1] giving me some wise counsel. I like questioning people who know what I do not know, Louise and you have always noticed it.

If I slipped quickly away from Paris it is because I was a little rushed at the last minute. Two hours before leaving Sabine I did not even know the times of the Geneva express, and it was Mme Howland who sent to her Swiss neighbour to find out. My regards to everyone. In a fortnight you will see me reappearing. Give me news of Rose Lemoinne[2] and our friends—Gounod prevented you from seeing Mme Weldon,[3] I already know that. Tell Mme Howland that I should like to know some other things.

I happened to get from Mr. d'Ideville a rather exaggerated note of introduction to the consul general at Naples, Mr. du Tour, whom you must know, and who is, I believe, particularly friendly with Meilhac and as a result with Rebouleau, who was with Meilhac (style Lippmann). I went to see my consul and he recommended a lawyer here. Tell Meilhac, if he writes to Mr. du Tour to thank him for the gracious way he received me, in spite of the ironically exaggerated introduction of Mr. d'Ideville.

Sigurd[4] is officer of the legion of honour! Will he remain on the repertoire because of that? You alone can guess.

[1] Permanent secretary to the Académie Française.
[2] Later Mme J. E. Blanche.
[3] Professional singer, friend of Gounod.   [4] Reyer.

114

There are not so many distinctive handkerchiefs here as I had hoped, it is necessary to go into the country. I should like to have nothing else to do.

And now your lecture with all the little points that you will have prepared so religiously quite alone or in the presence of Cavé or in the presence of Doucet himself. I have just written a lot, I am tired, I have nothing more to say. I now wish to get letters from France showing the interest that is, I think, my present due.

But I must not forget to tell you that Sickert signalled my arrival in Naples to a family Richmond from Australia, one of whose daughters appeared in profile in the watch of the unfortunate Barnes at Dieppe; that he begged me with his well known charm to go and see a delightful person to whom he had taught the art of respecting me; and that I went. It is very easy to go to Pausilippe by tram, to visit a young Australian in a bourgeois, Anglo-Italian pension in a wise, bewitching country. So I did it and I shall inform Sickert who will be touched. They examined me, holding in their hands a photograph of Sickert and myself, taken by Barnes at Dieppe. They really seemed to think I was better than on the paper. I am telling you. Write to me.

Calata Trinita Maggiore, Napoli. Italia.

99

To Bartholomé

Naples, 17 Jan. *1886*

Today, Sunday, I was to have gone to Pouzzoles on the Lac Fusaro, to Baia etc. to do a tour, my dear friend, to see what I had never seen in my journeys to Naples! It is raining and I am writing, which is not in any way disagreeable seeing it is to you that I am writing. Your wife, recognising my handwriting, will open this one too whilst you are busy with the commissions you do so well. We shall see each other again, I am coming back soon, I have no strength to negociate such a matter and my point insisted on here, is nothing but a simple landlords pilgrimage. You thought my letter very sad, and to a certain extent you are right. Interest and sentiment struggle within me in a strange way and I can but ill defend myself on these two points. I also have a horrible fear of lawyers or advocates. But who else could do the estimates? I am copying and translating so many deeds and contracts, so many papers, and one day I shall arrive in Paris with all the papers and fall into the arms of a Rouart or any other friend well versed in the questions I need. In the spring I shall return to Naples, better equipped. That seems to me to be the best thing. Only I have just wasted one month which could have been less painful.

They are not forgetting me in Paris, you are not the only one to write me, my good friend. But no one writes better or more affectionately than you do, not even the women. Young Jacques has had himself introduced to Mme Howland and his load of gossip will succeed there. *Nihil humanum* must be unbearable to bear. I am speaking of other times, for with the exception of the heart it seems to me that everything within me is growing old in proportion. And even this heart of mine has something artificial. The dancers have sewn it into a bag of pink satin, pink satin slightly faded, like their dancing shoes.

I am anxious to see your picture. How pretty the photo-

116

14. THE BALLET MASTER

15. SELFPORTRAIT

graphed drawing is that you gave me! But it is essential to do the same subject over again, ten times, a hundred times.[1] Nothing in art must seem to be chance, not even movement.

100

To Henri Rouart

Thursday, Paris, *1886*

Your sad and good letter did not need to be sent on. I am still in Paris, my dear friend.

In about a week's time I may go and spend a short time with my old bourgeois of the Orne,[2] and I need to do so more for the sake of my eyes than of my mind. It is not too bad in town if one likes it. And, at bottom, you know quite well I do rather like it.

One must continue to look at everything, the small and the large boats, the stir of people on the water and on the dry land too. It is the movement of people and things that distracts and even consoles if there is still consolation to be had for one so unhappy. If the leaves of the trees did not move, how sad the trees would be and we too! There is a tree in the garden of the neighbouring house which moves at each breath of wind. Well, its all very well my being in Paris in my almost dirty studio, I say to myself that this tree is delightful ...

[1] See annot. p. 265.   [2] Paul Valpinçon.

117

101

TO ALEXIS ROUART

Friday

MY DEAR FRIEND,

Your brother will most certainly not think of passing on this message to you. He has just told me that it would be better to write. Well, Thursday next, the 15 June, there will be a small housewarming 21, rue Pigalle, in the most beautiful apartment on the third floor that is to be found in the whole Quartier. Were your wife not to accompany you she would deliver you over to seductions of all kinds and would deprive herself of surprises, that I firmly believe to be delightful and would cause me uncalled for pain.—So once more, till Thursday at 9 o'clock, punctually, in a frockcoat.

Moreover I am coming to dine with you on Tuesday.

Your friend,
DEGAS

102

TO X . . . [1]

Undated

MONSIEUR,

Our friend Rouart wired the good news to me immediately, both proud and happy at your letter. The guilty party Rousset came to see me, as radiant as he had previously been crestfallen. He was given as serious a talking to as possible. He is deeply grateful to you, that

[1] This letter is a rough copy, smudged with ink, which was found amongst Degas' papers.

goes without saying, and he assured me that this service would make him your eternal debtor. I believe it as he says it, Monsieur.

There was a deal of impatience in you the other evening, and whilst you dealt my affection for that animal more blows than you perhaps intended, I thought, in spite of being no very subtle diplomat, that the best thing for me to do was to keep quiet, to excuse you and to wait.

Admit, Monsieur, that you think I was a little right. So you are less wicked than you say, than you wished to appear. There is, too, considerable *finesse* in the method of proving it to you.

When I have the pleasure of seeing you again, Monsieur, which pleasure the excellent Rouart will surely give me, I shall be better able to tell you how touched I am.

DEGAS

103

TO X ... [1]

Undated

I have received the 800 fr., my dear friend, and thank you. Speed up the framing.

Would you have the goodness to lend me *Les petites Modistes* for the exhibition?[2] You could send them with your brother's pictures.

Kind regards,
DEGAS

1.30

[1] Written with black crayons on notepaper with a small black border.

[2] Probably the 8th and last Impressionist exhibition (May–June 1886), at which Degas did exhibit the Pastel *Petites Modistes*.

119

104

TO FAURE

16 June 1886

MY DEAR MONSIEUR FAURE,

I receive your friendly summons and am going to start right away on your *Courses*. Will you come here towards the end of next week to see how it is progressing? The unfortunate thing is that I shall have to go and see some real racing again and I do not know if there will be any after the Grand Prix.

If it is finished I shall set to work on the *Blanchisseuse*.

In any case you will be able to see something of your own next Saturday, 24 June, between 3 and 6 o'clock.

Kind regards,

DEGAS

Thursday morning

105

TO FAURE

2 July 1886

MY DEAR MONSIEUR FAURE,

I shall need a few more days to finish your big picture of the Races. I have taken it up again and I am working on it.

A rather nasty trick that has been played on me, has just monopolized me for eight days on something other than your things. It was necessary to stop up a gap at once.

A few days more and you will have satisfaction.

DEGAS

Friday evening.

106

To Durand-Ruel

13 Aug. 1886

My dear Monsieur Durand-Ruel,

One delays coming to see the pastel, I am sending it to you. You will get another (of horses) and the little *Course* (in oils) with a background of mountains.

Please send me some money *this afternoon*. Try and give me half the sum each time I send you something. Once my fortunes have been restored I might well keep nothing for you and so free myself completely from debt. At the moment I am horribly embarrassed. It is for that reason that I was anxious to sell this particular pastel to someone other than yourself, so as to be able to keep all the money.

Kind regards,

Degas

2 o'clock.

107

To Faure

My dear Monsieur Faure,

I received the other day on an *open* telegram your request for a reply to your last letter.

It is getting more and more embarrassing for me to be your debtor. And if I do not terminate my debt it is because it is difficult for me to do so. This summer I set to work again on your pictures, particularly the one of the horses, and I had hoped to bring it to an end rapidly. But a certain Mr. B. judged it right to leave me saddled with a

121

drawing and a picture that he had ordered from me. In full summer this dead loss overwhelmed me. It was necessary to put aside all the things belonging to Mr. Faure in order to fabricate others which would enable me to live. I can only work for you in my spare moments and they are rare.

The days are short, little by little they will grow longer, and if one earns a little money one will be able to take up your work. I could enter into longer explanations. The ones I give you are the simplest and most irrefutable.

I beg you therefore to have a little more patience, I shall have some in finishing things which must swallow up my poor time gratuitiously and which love and respect for my art forbid me to neglect.

Accept, my dear Monsieur Faure, my sincere regards.

DEGAS

2 January 87.

108

TO MADAME FLEURY

Undated

DEAR MADAME,

So I replied neither to your good letter nor to the expectation that your poor protegé was inflicting on me. What he showed me is of no interest and my collection of Gavarni could gain nothing from it.

So your poor sister-in-law[1] is ill again and in view of what I saw the other day and in view of what Mlle Cassatt told me this morning she is bad. Poor woman, poor man! My hard heart melts all the same. They are very unhappy both of them.

[1] Madame Bartholomé (maiden name de Fleury) died in 1887.

122

When shall I have the pleasure of seeing you?

I shut myself up too much in my studio. I do not see the people I love often enough and I shall end up by suffering for it.

I press your hand,

Your friend,

DEGAS

Tuesday.

109

TO HENRY LEROLLE

2 Mar. 1887

This postponement, my dear Lerolle, may be a sorrow without being inconvenient. It suits me very well. So till Saturday 12.

I wanted to finish with a strong thought. After having waited for rather a long time, and without ceasing to be somewhat obscure, I address this to you: In loving nature we can never be quite sure whether she requites it.— What should I gain by expressing myself more clearly?

Kindest remembrances to Mme Lerolle and hoping to see you soon.

110

TO DURAND-RUEL

Undated

MY DEAR DURAND-RUEL,

Here is a small one, I shall send you the big one (*La Femme devant une Glace*) during the afternoon. I have only just this moment got the mirror.

123

If I do not come to the rue de la Paix before dinner I wish you would be good enough to put 1.500 francs aside for me for my rent of the 15 and I shall go and fetch them from you rue Constantinople to-morrow morning.

I had to do a pastel for Delorière, the dealer who let me have the Gavarnis. I sent it to him yesterday. I warned you of this infraction did I not?

Regards,

DEGAS

III

TO BARTHOLOMÉ

1888

MY DEAR FRIEND,

We shall go and dine with you on Monday which is better than Wednesday. We shall be there early to see the Christ.[1] Happy sculptor! I too should like ... but I have not done enough horses. The women must wait in their fountains.[2]

Regards,

DEGAS

Sunday morning.

[1] One of Bartholomé's first sculptures, it was done for the tomb of the first Mme Bartholomé at Bouillant, near Crépy-en-Valois.

[2] It is interesting to note that from this time on Degas had the idea of sculpturing women in fountains, an idea which he carried out later.

124

112

TO BARTHOLOMÉ

Undated

My dear friend and perhaps caster, I warn you that to-morrow, Saturday, there is an exhibition of Ingres drawings, a special exhibition. If you wish to go there come to the Studio at 12 o'clock, 12.30 or to the little Véfour until 1.30. I shall have a ticket, we shall go together. Before these marvels of the human mind we shall think of Raffaëlli, without otherwise speaking of him.

Regards,

DEGAS

Friday.

113

TO HENRI ROUART

Friday, *1888*

My dear friend, you are leaving Le Mans and I shall not have been there. Tell the colonel, the general even, seeing that at this moment they are one and the same person, that I am preparing for the school of Cauterets. Tillot must have written to you that poor Mlle Cassatt had a fall from her horse, broke the tibia of her right leg and dislocated her left shoulder. I met him two days later and told him the story; he was to have written to you the same evening. She is going on well, and here she is for a long time to come, first of all immobilized for many long summer weeks and then deprived of her active life and perhaps also of her horsewoman's passion.

The horse must have put its foot in a hole made by the rain on soft earth. HE[1] hides his daughter's *amour-propre* and above all his own.

I wager you never thought of asking if anyone at Le Mans owned a copy of *Thousand and one Nights*? What delightful moments you would have spent, perhaps as delightful as mine.

To-morrow I shall be in attendance at Crépy-en-Valois, for the erection of Bartholomé's Christ, but I am returning in the evening. The examination for Cauterets is hard.

I am eager to see you again, a new man through camp life in a room, enriched by some young and firm and restrained aquarelles.

Tillot, secretary of the Barye exhibition, complains of being a sinecurist. He has nothing but our admiration in his cash box.

Greetings to the general, colonel *malgré lui*. Au revoir.

114

To Henri Rouart

HOTEL D'ANGLETERRE, CAUTERETS
about 1888

If you were here you would be hot and without pain in your shoulder, my dear friend. It is possible to draw trees everywhere without any danger, provided one does not go into the water. One can even confirm from the perspec-

[1] Miss Cassatt's father.

126

tive of their pictures that the Van Eycks and others whom you saw at Bruges (Lafond read me your letter) and whom I know from Paris, drew all kinds of trees, of flowers, of mountains from a good window.[1]

Greetings to the wise . . .

115

To Bartholomé

HOTEL D'ANGLETERRE
Cauterets, 30 Aug.

. . . I am avoiding the Maître de Forge but all the same I shall go to the Mascotte, for the first time I give you my oath. But preferable to everything is the real Punch and Judy show on the Esplanade in the evening, I attach myself to it but I dare not answer and speak to Punch like the children sitting on the benches, whose advice Punch takes or scorns according to his mood. It is one of the best things for the mind at Cauterets, perhaps the only thing[2] . . .

116

To Ludovic Halévy

HOTEL D'ANGLETERRE
Cauterets, 6 Sept. 1888

My dear Halévy,

I am writing to you out of boredom and to tell you absolutely nothing at all. And I am using the familiar form of address for the sake of intimacy in order to

[1] Rouart often walked great distances in order to find motifs for his landscapes. See annot. p. 265.

[2] Duranty had written such plays for his *Théâtre de Marionnettes*, published in 1863 and preceded by a remarkable introduction.

127

diminish the distance that separates us, perhaps also from a feeling of friendship. My congratulations on Elie's[1] success for you, Elie himself, his mother and Daniel[2] too.

Where have they deported me to! I take immense care to drink according to the orders of Evariste Michel.[3] I am hardly enjoying myself, all alone as I am and reading little. All this instead of shutting myself up no matter where and chewing arabic gum of the finest quality, as you so wisely repeated to me!

Madame de Mailly[4] is here in person. She is leaving tomorrow. I sent her my Turkish respects by way of a certain Russian whose acquaintance I made here, through the act of a general of the artillery, that goes without saying. But with my discretion, I made no effort to join her, fearing her ill-temper and above all what is called her beauty. Yesterday I met her in front of the new César (Rocher and Rieumiset combined). She was most gracious, charged me, if I were writing to you, with all her friendly wishes for you and Louise. But during this speech I was looking at her and I thought her strangely thin and changed.

Must I tell you about a certain Punch who is the only noble minded distraction that I have here! Can you imagine a piece at cross purposes, disunited and often improved by the interruptions and the demands of the children, more cruel, more fierce, more logical than himself, Punch? There was (she has left now) a little girl who was a great trial to Punch in the pursuit of his business. She directed the play. The man from Auvergne yielded too.

[1] Eldest son of Ludovic Halévy.
[2] Second son of Ludovic Halévy.
[3] Doctor at Cauterets, a friend of the Halévy's.
[4] Countess de Mailly-Nesle, famous for her beauty and for her voice. She later married the famous singer, Jean de Reszké.

128

Write me a line, my dear friend, to distract me, to instruct me and to please me.

Greetings to Louise and to the two young men.

DEGAS

117

TO OCTAVE MAUS

Paris, 8 Dec. 1888

DEAR MONSIEUR,

I received your two most flattering and winning letters and I admit that I hesitated a lot before answering them. Permit me to decline the proposition you put to me,[1] I have too many reasons for staying away and I have a fancy that I cannot overcome to confine myself to this country.

So please be good enough to make my sincere apologies to your friends, dear Monsieur, and believe me yours very sincerely

DEGAS

118

TO BARTHOLOMÉ

Cauterets, 9 Sept.

I hear him, I see him, all red with anger and[2] ... saying the famous 'Women think they can do everything,' which he will please have the goodness to repeat at my injunction. I continue to thank you for your good letters, my dear friend, and when I recognize them on the green

[1] To exhibit at the *Libre Esthétique* in Brussels.
[2] Illegible word.

baize cloth in the hotel office I know I am about to spend a pleasant moment. But, for all that they are not going to release me before the 15th, still the whole week to spend, it is high time I was liberated, it really is a bit hard. Lafond came the other day to surprise me, and what struck him most in me as persisting through all the bad treatments, my magesterial air.

Why do you go mainly at night on your wandering jew excursions? To put me off them perhaps? All the same I regretted very much not being with you instead of being at no. 132 of this asylum. My own cross is laid on a table d'hôte and I swear to you the two ruffians, though they have the faces of advocates or landlords, do not speak to me, do not confide their affairs to me, so wicked is my face. Finally, this is the end, I shall go no more to Cauterets deprived of all human aid!

I had at last written to Mr. de Fleury, a word of congratulation on his book. He replied at once with a very affectionate letter.

How can one look after oneself for anything so sensitive as the respiratory channels, style admitted, in a country where the weather changes every instant? Yesterday I could hardly talk. I had caught cold in the fog and in the rain and I already saw myself interned and ill in these parts. Foot baths at César, monkshood, Dr. Franck's health grains, were prescribed and carried out. Evariste Michel thinks it will be nothing, I have just seen him again this minute. The *Thousand and one Nights* calm me, instruct me and raise me to the heights of wisdom. Read the story of Cogia Hassan the ropemaker. It is the book of Job.

Go to, you could easily write me once more, I deserve it well. When writing to Mlle Cassatt, 16 rue d'Avon at

130

Fountainebleau, I could not resist telling her of the humiliation of our Raffaëlli by the Hottentote lady.—She replied and amongst other things she tells me that, whilst riding in the forest and having got lost among the rocks, her mare shied and that she thought she saw a small animal moving in the grass and that home again she saw her steed's leg already swollen. It was a viper. It appears that a viper is healthier for animals than it is for us and that it does not kill.

It is Paris-Lyons-M that kills. Never will they understand derailing will they? They are all from the school[1] . . . but only Captain Baschet, who must be from it, understood. He said at once 'I am lost, goodbye.' Should one be satisfied with statistics and say as certain people do, that there are less dead on the railways than on the stage coaches or else should one impose enormous fines on the big railway companies? My head is not strong enough at the moment to decide.

I shall tell you some things about Punch. It is too long. And then, with the cold I have caught and the cold outside I shall have to stay in the hotel in the evenings. And he himself, my poor friend, he too will have to leave for lack of children who do not catch cold on his benches.

Should I have done the masterly drawing of the mountains, I should have died, so you will not regret it, neither shall I.

They were seen at Montmartre, in Sweden
(Twice) To the North, to the South and then elsewhere
        Lud. Halévy and ?
    The children asked their mothers
(Twice) Oh, who are these two travellers.

[1] The Polytechnic school, one of Degas' bêtes noirs.

131

There is no more time to write to Clermont. Evariste Michel himself must write to him.

Shall I tell you something that I am very much afraid of? It is that I shall find the Christ[1] finished. Greetings to Fleury and to the Venetian.[2]

Sincerely yours,

DEGAS

119

TO BARTHOLOMÉ

13 June 1889

. . . I have worked the little wax a lot.[3] I have made it a socle with linen dipped in a more or less well mixed plaster . . .

120

TO BARTHOLOMÉ

Undated

. . . Love to both of you. I neglect you badly. I had some wearying articles to do, I still have some to do, and they needs must have, alas, bad as they are, the best that is in me.

Till Thursday,

DEGAS

---

[1] Bartholomé's sculpture.   [2] Zandomeneghi.
[3] Still the little dancer of 14 years, exhibited for the first time at the fifth Impressionist Exhibition in 1880. See annot. p. 263.

132

To Bartholomé

Wednesday
14 Aug. 1889.

The hotel de France is, Lafond says so, the *good* hotel. He has just left for Pau an hour ago . . .

Mme Alexis Rouart is at the hotel d'Angleterre with her niece and I for my part am in no. 11, very beautiful room with balcony and two windows. Extremely simple society, aristocracy from the provinces, right-minded people, a few signs of the cross before eating the soup. No one asked me my profession. Can it be that I look it? See here, Bartholomé, do not deceive me.

I had to give Cherfils the slip and Bagnères-de-Bigarre. It will be difficult to escape him on my return, at Pau, after 3 days of friendship. And yet it is necessary to start work again and the fortune that Manzi[1] places at my feet, as a carpet.

Talking of old goats we have here the Barónne de P. a discarded one of Haas,[2] walking just now with Mme d'A., a discarded one of Haas. If he himself were to arrive unexpectedly, what a new note in my *good* hotel!

Apart from Bas Relief itself, should not sculpture be the unique art to give the idea of forms which all the same are deceptive in the relief? It is the relief that spoils everything, that is most deceptive, and yet it is in that that everyone believes. This will take me a long way. . . .

---

[1] See annotations, p. 266.
[2] Charles Haas 1832–1902. Brilliant figure in Parisian society. (See annotations, p. 266.)

To Boldini[1]

Cauterets, Thursday
August 1889

I have just this moment received your excellent telegram, my dear companion, and everything seems to me to be going well. From Pau where I shall be on the 2 and shall stay the 3, 4 and 5, I shall give you instructions, after having talked to my friends Cherfils, great experts on journeys to Spain. Lafond, whose advice is so precious, will be absent from the secret session. He left for Touraine yesterday, Wednesday, with plans of his own that we shall never know. The weather is very fine and hot in the mountains. We shall, without the slightest doubt, be roasted in the planes of Castille, but the museums are always cool. I am stuffing myself with Spanish ideas by reading the guide, the Journey of de Amicis, and a handbook of bull-fighting that Lafond sent me this morning.

You will receive the information at 41, Boulevard Berthier, on Wednesday or Thursday. By your leaving Paris on Thursday evening and my leaving Pau on Friday morning we could meet at Bayonne at 10.48 and set off immediately for Spain without any wait in Bonnat's country. And that through your having taken the 8.20 train in the evening, as it would appear from your wire to be your intention to do. But wait for a letter from Pau regarding the tickets to take.

[1] Jean Boldini, a portrait painter, born 1845 at Ferrara, died in Paris 1931.

During your interim stay in Paris try to go and visit Bartholomé and ask him if he has any observation mission to confide to us.

See you soon,

DEGAS

123

TO BOLDINI

HOTEL DE FRANCE, CAUTERETS
Sunday, *August 1889.*

MY DEAR BOLDINI,

You insisted on being warned, you are. The journey to Madrid will take place about the 5 September. My treatment ends on Monday the 2 September. The Tuesday, Wednesday and Thursday I shall spend at Pau and on the evening of the 5 or the morning of the 6 I shall leave Pau to wait for you at Bayonne or Hendaye, that is to say the frontier.

I know you to be modest and incapable of taking advantage of a situation or a title of any kind, President of the Italian jury or any other, to demand special consideration. You will travel incognito, will you not? So get down to it and consult a good railway guide and brood over the advantages of return tickets or circular routes (very little circular). As a matter of fact I shall send you a carefully thought out written itinerary from Pau. But first of all let me know your plans at once. You can write to me here until Sunday September 1.

Lafond has been most loyal. He is leaving for La

135

Touraine on Tuesday and will be in Paris towards the 20. He has engraved the head of his portrait by you. The Verdi is finished and is not bad.

There will still be the possibility of seeing a small bull fight in Madrid. You will complete your education, begun academically rue Pergolese, etc. etc., if you are really coming.

Hoping to receive your orders (as they say in business), I beg you to receive my sentiments of curiosity.

DEGAS

124

TO BARTHOLOMÉ

Cauterets, 19 Aug. 89.
Monday

Henri, Baron d'Ernemon, my neighbour on the left at table, 65 years old, after the departure of his neighbour to the left, has attacked me. All his thoughts, in spite of the enormous pieces of everything and in particular of rocquefort which are hunks, he communicates to me incessantly. And he thinks like Arnal on every subject. I weep over it and he loves to see me weep on account of him. As a matter of course he names all the people he has known. Such a thing happened to him at his Château de Neuilly, near and between Pacy-sur-Eure and . . . whilst talking to Mme de Boisgelin, the younger, Mlle de . . . Another thing with a prostitute of Amiens. With it all, this man is a very good looking man, and his broad shoulders have supported a worthless life. He was the intimate friend of

136

16. DIEGO MARTELLI

17. DIEGO MARTELLI

Janvier de la Motte, his prefect of course. It is impossible that you do not know, even through Mr. de Fleury, what this creature is worth. 'Here is another good one. If you know it stop me.' One would have to be a policeman to stop him. I come upon him at the corner of the refreshment room and it is always he who attacks first. However, he has tact; he left me after lunch, he reserves me, he knows his audience.

Langlès, the big biscuit manufacturer, the neighbour on the right, certainly has a more solid mentality than the baron. Did I tell you that he lives Avenue Kleber, that he has lost his eldest grand-daughter, that he left Paris out of sadness and installed his family in an estate at Pau, he himself having to go to his factory there every winter? And he even went to draw models at the Academy de Colarossi, where Courtois, or Blanc, or Dagnan Bouveret, or Flameng corrected his work. I had to tell him that I was a painter and he was not frightened by it.

I am writing to you, Mr. Bartholomé, even though it is 5.30 o'clock, the hour of the promenade, because it is pouring with rain. And I think I deserve one or other of those good letters to amuse me and wait for the end. Madame Howland and her pianist went to see you, I know, and admired and envied your passion for art and for work. And one must say there is some reason for it.

Forain had done a drawing of Mme Prudence. You must remember it. I can visualize it but I have forgotten the title. She knows how to make you love the future, does she not, without breathing a word about it? But what is even more simple is the fact that one is in the same boat oneself.

I am still thinking of a journey to Spain and of a real

137

bull fight. Should I get that flashy dago Boldini to come? Lafond, will he follow? Will I myself have the courage not to return to Paris without further exposing my life? Alas! I have still 13 days to go and time not to make a decision.

But I almost deprived you of the pleasure of knowing that Haas may arrive in 8 or 10 days, and that the attitude he will take towards me, whether he sees me or cuts me (like a corn in the rue de La Paix) will cost him something or will cost him nothing. He knows that I do not see, and that when I see I am indifferent. Will he have a plan and the courage to carry it out? You know how funny they are with other men, these ladies' men.

Have you ever been to see the water railway at the Invalides with the engineer Manzi, the rich amateur? Try to go there and to tell me about it.

My regards to Fleury (from the sea) and to your Italians. Do not do too much of that sculpture before my arrival.

'Deuced weather,' I said to the baron, followed immediately by: 'I prefer it to the guillotine.'

Sincerely yours,

DEGAS

125

TO BARTHOLOMÉ

Madrid, Sunday, 8 Sept. 1889.
Hotel de Paris, 2 o'clock afternoon

You could write me a line, my dear Bartholomé, to this address for our return from Andalousie. For want of you,

138

whose absence I, and even Boldini, feel to such a degree, that at every moment we say 'if Bartholomé were here, how happy he would be!' you could tell us how your brother is, what possibility there still is for you to join us.

Arrived this morning about 6.30 (you would have liked to arrive at a time that suited you better, for instance 4 o'clock, you would not have been able to). From 9 o'clock until about midday, visit to the museum, back at the hotel and lunch (since we have been in Spain we eat admirably and people always spoke of food poisoning), a heat that presages something incredible at Andalousie. The bull fight, for which we are preparing, will not take place until 4.30. They themselves expect that the sun will not wither them. Nothing, no nothing can give the right idea of Velasquez. We shall speak of it all the same on my return, with the other things.

I beg you once again, my dear friend, try and join us at Madrid. You could economize more than we do, you are tougher and less exacting than we are. Reckon it out with the timetable, and I bet that with 300 francs you could get a return, travelling second class. We should imitate you. Boldini keeps the accounts and you can form some idea of the need he feels to spend. I shall send you a wire from Seville, so that you can mark us on the map.

It seems possible to set foot in Marrocco, but only for a few hours.

I am going to sleep a little, which I did too little last night (18 hours from Irun to Madrid). Met Bonnat on the outside of the omnibus at Biarritz.

Sincerely yours with all my heart,

DEGAS

139

To Bartholomé

CONTINENTAL HOTEL,
TANGIERS, MOROCCO
Wednesday, 18 Sept. *1889*

One can do nothing less than write to you, my dear Bartholomé, from such a spot. Can you imagine me on a mule, taking part in a cavalcade that was led by a guide in a violet silk robe on the sand of the sea, in the dust and along the paths of the surrounding countryside, and then across Tanger?

Another year will we be able to do the same journey that you gave me the sarrow of doing alone, or very nearly? The guide in the silk robe knows French, but it is not yours.

One loves in nature those people who have not been unworthy to appreciate it. I tell you this because Delacroix passed here.

The boat brought us here under a grey sky, but there were all the same in this grey more pearls than slate.

I have nothing to tell you, I am writing to you to date my friendship from Tangiers. In a week at the most I shall be rue de Chaillot. To-morrow, return to Cadiz, from whence we leave Friday at 5 o'clock for Granada. After this last effort one can re-read *Thousand and one Nights*. I read in a book that here the families still preserve their landowners' titles in Spain and the keys of their houses through the centuries through which I am passing in such bad company.

Kind regards rue de la Pompe and very sincerely yours with all my heart.

DEGAS

140

127

TO CLAUDE MONET

1889–1890.

MY DEAR MONET,

Please forgive me. I am answering less promptly than I should. Please put me down on your list for the sum of one hundred francs. You will let me know when I should send them to you.[1]

Greetings,

DEGAS

128

TO BARTHOLOMÉ

CABINET DE MANZI, RUE FOREST
Thursday, *1890*

Manzi as a hussar with a Basque beret to which he gives Italian forms. Lafond, near the fire pretends to be without commissions.

One demands news of you.

I say that you are coming Saturday.

Manzi has sold the head of a woman by Zandomeneghi who will continue to conceal his satisfaction from us for a little while.

So come back on Saturday.

Thank your sister very much. She will applaud other attempts in the spring.

[1] This refers to the subscription organised by Monet to get Manet's *Olympia* into the Louvre.

141

129

To Manzi

Undated

After leaving you yesterday, I met Mme Strauss[1] (Halévy's cousin) and I was forced to abandon you for tomorrow. It is almost the only day that this person, in demand on all sides, has free and simple, and I had neglected her so much that I had to yield. I was dragged to a fashionable dressmakers where, like a Béraud,[2] I assisted at the fitting of a most effective toilette.

I went to the rue Forest at 4 o'clock without meeting you and I am forced to write to you.

Kind regards,

DEGAS

Saturday, half past 6.

130

To Monsieur Brebion[3]

13 April 1890.

Here are the few alterations which, at the advice of my friend and counsellor Bartholomé, I should be obliged if you would make in your lease.

Have the goodness to add apropos the payment in money *in gold and silver* and not otherwise or in *notes of the Bank of France.*

[1] See annotations, p. 267.
[2] Jean Béraud, popular painter of small Parisian scenes. He also painted scenes from the life of Christ in contemporary costumes.
[3] Degas' landlord at 37 rue Victor Massé.

142

I should like to remain free, as regards the insurance, from opportunism and from the company. It would be equally distasteful to me to be submitted to your inspection of the receipts and to have to bear this double *policing*.

I am content with a simple lease, drawn up between us. If for your special business you need a legalized lease it will be up to you to pay for it. That is perfectly straightforward.

You must make a brief survey of the state of the premises which is not adequate. The moment the repairs are finished, that is to say in two or three days, I hope, we shall make a little inspection together and see on the spot exactly, or approximately what there is. *Entirely renovated* is a little exaggerated. I did not ask for anything more and I have made concessions to you. I should not like to give anything more.

Finally, in case of a break, that is to say the non-renewal of the lease, three months must suffice. Why six months?

Ah, you really have helped me to earn a little peace in your charming apartment. Do not let us quarrel any more, I beg of you. I am a quiet and solvent tenant, do not ask more from me.

Hoping to see you soon. Let us finish in a day or two, and please accept my compliments.

DEGAS

To M. Le Comte Lepic
supplier of good dogs, at Berck

Undated

Dear Monsieur,

I have been twice too satisfied with your deliveries not to turn to you once again. Could you not either from your kennels and apartments, or from your friends and acquaintances, find me a small griffon, thoroughbred or not (dog or bitch), and send it to me to Paris if an opportunity arises or by carrier. As regards the price I shall not consider that further than you did. However if you should wish to draw on me for a sum exceeding 50 centimes, I should be grateful if you would warn me some months in advance as is always the custom in these parts.

Please accept, Monsieur le Comte, my sincere regards.

E. Degas

I think it in good taste to warn you that the person who desires this dog is Mlle Cassatt, that she approached me, who am known for the quality of my dogs and for my affection for them as for my old friends etc etc. I also think that it is useless to give you any information about the asker, whom you know for a good painter, at this moment engrossed in the study of the reflection and shadow of chairs or dresses, for which she has the greatest affection and understanding, not that she resigns herself to the use of only *green and red* for this effect which I consider the only salvation, etc. etc. etc.

This distinguished person whose friendship I honour, as you would in my place, asked me to recommend to you the youth of the subject. It is a young dog that she needs, so that he may love her.

By sending with the dog, if you do send the dog, you would give an appreciable pleasure to your requester, by sending with this dog some news of your health and of your noble pursuits.[1]

132

To Bartholomé

Received at Angoulême, 29 April 1890[2]
Monday evening.

I have a vague idea, my dear friend, that Thursday morning, about 10 o'clock, as your message says, you will find me out, at least in my Studio. In the first place since yesterday I am sleeping at the house, and then, the papers announcing that there will be no further performances of *Salammbô* after Sunday of this month, I can see myself leaving Wednesday morning at 8.15 for my destination. The danger of Thursday might be found again at Brussels, a people of strikers. Moreover, the whole question does not lie there. There are also the arms of Mme Caron which might be long enough to cover me.

The calicoes from Angoulême impressed you, I see. But the society of Angoulême? Mme de Bargeton? The lady, who in a château in the surroundings has the sole score of *Salammbô*, has she also a dress? This dress is perhaps of the same material as the pattern?

Furnishing continues to preoccupy me. Portier has seen

---

[1] See annotations, p. 265.   [2] Note by Bartholomé.

the carpet remnant and above all the famous one, the carpet of the virtuoso, the expensive one.

In spite of a feeling of extravagance which is a mixture of taste and of senile grotesquerie, it is still in the shop where I shall not set foot without your eyes. A new purchase by the Louvre under the eye of Portier, but of no consequence.

You can feel it, the carpet holds me. I am drawn to the carpet like the cat. During the time of the crusades what might one not have found as booty or by chance!

Dinner at the Fleury's on Saturday with Mlle Cassatt. Japanese exhibition at the Beaux Arts. A fireman's helmet on a frog. Alas! Alas! taste everywhere.

Thank your sister and the colonel for their wishes. See you soon. Manzi whom I have just left has a frock coat with silk lapels. Everything, everything in this world has a *sacré* meaning.

Kind regards,

DEGAS

133

TO THORNLEY[1]

Cauterets, 28 April.
HOTEL D'ANGLETERRE.

I had a fresh attack of bronchitis and after having stayed indoors for a while in Paris they sent me here, my dear Mr. Thornley.

Before persecuting you about the stones, I shall con-

[1] Painter and engraver, who published a series of lithographs of pictures and pastels of Degas.

146

gratulate you on your marriage, here you are a happy boy. Moreover you were proceeding at such a pace that one could not help suspecting something as important.

A few days after your flight they brought me two proofs from Béquet (women trying on hats). I told them to stop the printing and warned them that I would go to the printing office. It was impossible for me to go there, also to return to Rouart with your drawing on transfer paper. I wanted to make a few alterations on this latter one; and I scarcely regret not having done so as you were not there. I shall be in Paris about the 15 September and we shall get it finished.

You were in too much of a hurry, my dear Mr. Thornley. Things of art must be done at leisure. But your impatience is now fully clear to me.

Yours very sincerely,

DEGAS

134

To Bartholomé

Cauterets, HOTEL DE FRANCE.
16 August *1890*.

. . . So you will not be there when young Richaud, 1st flutist, perhaps accompanied by old Dihau, 1st basoonist, will play in a spot I shall have chosen and whose style will please me, the beginning of the Champs-Elysees act of Orpheus for me.

Sincerely yours,

DEGAS

147

135

To Bartholomé

Cauterets, 18 Aug. *1890*

. . . Little Richaud is having the music for the little concert for wood winds sent to him from Paris. I have a feeling that I shall be very much moved by it. Provided that Tillot knows nothing about it and does not come! . . .

136

To Bartholomé

HOTEL D'ANGLETERRE
Cauterets, 24 August.

I have just written to Rouart, I am a little tired, I shall write you a long letter another time, my dear friend. Well, Lafond was waiting for me at Pau, having come from Oloron, and the next morning, Wednesday, we both set off for Cauterets. Wait at Lourdes, until 2 o'clock. There was a pilgrimage. All kinds of moving things and made for you. You would never have forgotten, as I shall also know how to, a sick woman, dying, on a mattress laid across a char-à-banc; beside her her family returning from the cave. Miracles of the body or of the soul, or physical or mystic reactions, what things were painted on their faces. The pilgrims, much better, for the most part than the administration of pilgrimages, a little more simple. Zouaves of the pope doing duty as litter bearers; with my bad eyes, I missed everything you would have seen.

Here I have begun to drink.

It is very fine and very hot. I had promised you some drawings of mountains, and I was a bit too hasty. There are no very attractive forms here. We are closed in and nothing attracts me so far.

All the same it will be necessary to find distraction. If I can judge by these two days this treatment will be long-drawn-out. They say that Marguerite de Navarres wrote her tales here, to distract herself. I shall not be able to do as much, moreover I have never read them. Met no one to talk to a little freely. Why did you choose this moment to do sculpture? We possess Sarah Bernhardt, she has only Damala with her, her repatriated husband. We had Carolus Duran, in a costume worthy of himself and made for Chili, or for glory.

Write to me. Regards to the Venetian.

Sincerely yours,

DEGAS

Well, I saw Evariste Michel yesterday, to whom the Autruchien (sic) Clermont had not written.

137

TO BARTHOLOMÉ

Cauterets, Thursday
28 Aug. 1890.

I had much difficulty in reading the few pencilled thoughts that came from Diénay[1] with the portrait of Car-

1 At the Côte d'Or, where the painter Jeanniot, friend of Degas and Bartholomé, had a château.

149

not. And I saw you at Bourgogne as a friend carried away by the need to move, for yourself, but not for the dog. To take a dog to the country, for him to have a holiday instead of his master, that is true merit. Here, near la Raillère, ground has been hired for a pack of dogs who were hot at Pau, by an Englishman who has not, I believe, left Pau. So you are two. Tillot is, at the moment, Tillot for the ladies. How often does one not see him at the side of Mme Alice Kerr, artist of the theatre, having played second soubrettes at Montpellier, and supposed to play them soon at Lyons! He has suffered for good and all. Glasses conceal the ardours, with glasses one devours with the eyes. He has ceased to bore us, it is we who bore him. We pity him and it is the height of pleasure; but he has not had the lady, I guarantee; he is miserly, he wishes to offer something other than money. Everything is written on his exasperated person.

I shall leave here for Pau Sunday or Monday evening to shut myself up with Cherfils for two or three days. From there it is a question of going to Geneva where my brother Achille, who is no better, is waiting for me. From Geneva you have guessed without showing it too much that we could meet at Dijon, to go and spend a day at Diénay by Is-sur-Tille. We can bring back the dog and God's will would be done.

I was afraid of bronchitis, everything was shaping for it, it was avoided. What a terrible climate. It is raining at the moment. The mountain fête, postponed from Sunday to today, has been postponed to the first fine day, so says the crier on his drum ...

... Did I tell you that I have a neighbour at table, a friend of Lenhart (sic), who posed in the picture

150

le Bonheur et le Dessin?[1] He reproaches Lenhart, not without a certain wisdom, with always having an idea when he does a picture. Delauny[2] is here, I met him this morning and he told me that Mme Straus had just deposited Meilhac at Louchon, she was driving herself and herself injured her face. Meilhac has an attack of gout . . .

. . . Yesterday, the audition in the happy place of my choice! Well, I must tell you, this penetrating air, would it have moved me more, if the flute had been accompanied? No. It would have moved me, this flute, far from nature, on a painted canvas, because the presence of nature is insipid in a work of such art and also, if the idea of happiness must make me cry, it is when I am unhappy and at the theatre.

Amen,

DEGAS

138

TO HENRI ROUART

Cauterets, 11 September.

I am coming back, it is ending, my dear friend. And if ever I begin again, let it not be like this all alone, and so late! I may say that I am counting not the days but the hours.

One must love nature more than I do to stand a cure at Cauterets. But, sacré morning, I should love her did she

[1] This picture, painted by Max Leenhardt is now in the museum at Sète.

[2] The painter Delaunay, friend of Mme Straus. The portrait which he painted of her is now in the Louvre.

151

not threaten me every moment with her ills. You know how to brave her, but you know the feeling.

I shall be at my post from Friday week on, if you are at yours. I have seen some very beautiful things through my anger, and what consoles me a little, is that through my anger I do not stop looking ...

139

To Bartholomé

De Cauterets, *undated*

... I am thinking of my fortified enclosure where I am going to expiate a sentence of 10 months of delicious work.

Why are you not fonder of grey marble? You would come here to hew on the spot and through simple inclined planes we should make Egyptian purity descend to the verge of glory.

Sincerely yours,

Degas

The following letters refer to a journey through Burgundy made by Degas and Bartholomé in a tilbury drawn by a white horse. In common with all the ones addressed to the family Halévy, they are preserved at the Bibliothèque de L'Institut de France in the collection of autographs of Ludovic Halévy given to the institute by his sons (Ms. 4.483). They are preceded by the following note in Ludovic Halévy's hand:

'Tuesday morning the 30 September, Degas and Bartholomé arrive at Montgeron in the tilbury harnessed with the white horse.

152

18. MISS CASSATT AT THE LOUVRE

19. MISS CASSATT AT THE LOUVRE

They lunch at Montgeron and leave at two o'clock. We accompany them on the Melun road as far as the Pyramide.'

140

TO MADAME LOUISE HALÉVY
AT MONTGERON

Friday morning, 26 Sept. 90

We shall not be at the heights of Montgeron to-morrow, Saturday, about 11 o'clock, my dear Louise. I am pretty sure we shall be shaken. I am warning you for greater safety. For your part you might have your wheels greased. If only this magnificent weather, a little too fresh, continues. Moreover, all the world has its eyes fixed on us. Greetings to all the world.

DEGAS

141

TO GEORGES JEANNIOT

Sunday morning *1890*

The time is approaching; a white horse is crossing the forest of Senart, and behind him by him two old men are being drawn, one of whom, still a little younger, is holding a whip, seated a little higher. He, it appears, knows just where he is going. He does not believe the peasants, who never tell the truth about the way. He says that he who knows how to read a map should travel with his eyes closed. For a whole week maps had been stuck on the walls of the damp place,[1] and he studied them with a little

[1] Studio of Bartholomé in a garden in the rue de Chaillot.

153

rolling instrument in a dial, which was to prepare the varied route. He who has drawn a straight line and who wishes to follow it will not drink, say the scriptures.

We shall leave about midday. The white horse is intact, so is the tilbury, so are the two men, but less so, thank heavens!

We shall thus appear to be verifying, revising, for a mission, the map of the general staff, in military areas of the second line.

At bottom we have no other wish than to see again the enchanted palace where the gold ring was almost lost which the little princess Henriette,[1] the most beautiful republican princess in existence, dropped carelessly, advised as she was by the genie disguised as a Scotch terrier,[2] who had persuaded her that in this way she would break the spell and be able to refurnish the castle in one morning.[3]

He who scorches the roads with a white horse at the rate of ten leagues an hour, say the scriptures, is certain to arrive in a short week at the place unknown to the horse and familiar to the two old men. Of all the people in the secret of this displacement not one hesitated to proclaim the good sense of the two friends that you, dear Madame, and also your captain have the good fortune and the inconvenience of possessing. Notices sent out en route will enable you to follow us on the map and to see us approaching perfectly happy.

[1] Madame Georges Jeanniot.
[2] Scotch terrier that Degas liked to pretend was a genie.
[3] This château is a huge property situated on the highest spot of the village of Diénay.

154

142

TO MADAME LOUISE HALÉVY

29 Sept. 90.
Monday 10.30.

It is for to-morrow, Tuesday, for certain. So, my dear Louise, around 11.30 the white horse will be at the gate. Will you have the courage by such weather, not to go at least as far as Montereau to-morrow? The Jeanniots must have received an exaggerated letter this morning, which will keep them on the look out.

Greetings,

DEGAS

143

TO LUDOVIC HALÉVY

Tuesday evening 30 Sept. 90.

Evidently animals think and speak, particularly amongst themselves. Bartholomé noticed that our white assumed in the stable an air of vigorous roguishness towards your noble servant.

At the exit he took on, behind the other, a vexed and impetuous air—after the obelisk, the isolation and the sight of an enormous straight line calmed him. He slowed down to a walk too often. He acted exhausted in a town he did not wish to leave again. He has just devoured.[1]

[1] After this letter card the addresses, written in advance, are in Ludovic Halévy's writing.

144

To Ludovic Halévy

30 Sept. 90
Melun, 6.30

He is tired, we think only of him, Oats are everything, say the scriptures, they are better than a good word. Continuation to-morrow.[1]

145

To Alexis Rouart

Lettercard, stamped 1.10.90
Melun, 6.30 morning
Wednesday.

You see we are going. The white horse eats oats; in half an hour he will take us to Montereau. Everything depends on him, so we think only of him. If he weakens, we must weaken too. But he is likely to astonish us, said his flatterer and his coachmen in chorus yesterday morning at Ivry, which we left yesterday about 9 3/4.

Greetings to society and to you too.

Degas

146

To Ludovic Halévy

1st October, 90.
Montereau. Wednesday, 12.30

Everything goes like clockwork. He appeared this morning without animation at half past six. He left feebly.

[1] This card is not in Degas' writing.

156

There was nothing wrong with him. He had slept too much. Near Valence and in the wood we passed some char-à-bancs (one of them a cart, in which a Louis XV chair with red material confined an old man) full of people in black who must have been a funeral party seeing that they all looked exceedingly happy. He himself, he sensed Montereau from more than a league away, old stager that he is. The real Grand Monarch is here. Here is the real lunch, only I may tell you that sheep's foot is the thing best calculated to estrange you from calve's head. Everywhere praise of the horse, particularly in the stables. He is guaranteed to us from hour to hour. 'You have had him a long time', said the stable boy to Bartholomé. 'He was born at my place', he replied. Alas! it is only two days that we have him! What would we not have done already if we had had him in our days of maturity! Left at 4 o'clock for the continuation.

147

To LUDOVIC HALÉVY

2 October 90
Sens. Thursday, about 1.30.
Montereau, Hôtel du Grand Monarque
(the real one)
LUNCH
Sheep's foot.
Fried Gudgeon.
Sausage and mash (admirable).
Beefsteaks with cress.
Cheese, fruit, biscuits (admirable).

M   157   D.I.

The horse made a fine descent on Montereau.
Left at 3.30 for Villeneuve-la-Guyard.
There, continue to descend to the Hotel de la Poste.

DINNER

Panada with milk.
Brains melted butter.
Jugged hare.
Leg of mutton, mixed beans (famous).
Salad.
Mixed dessert.
Light red wine.

Left this morning at 7 o'clock.
No more thoughts, one eats too much. Each meal 3 francs.

148

To Ludovic Halévy

2 October 90
Cerisiers, 7 o'clock, Thursday

And to think that one could return to the town to pursue a ridiculous ideal!

The distance from the towns to the big market-towns has been calculated from the measure of a horse's strength.

149

To Ludovic Halévy

3 October 90
Saint-Florentin 1.30, Friday

No possibility of eating a cutlet in the province, what is good on a cutlet goes to Paris.

158

Bartholomé is the right man. Beneath that trappist's beard of his is the heart of a coachman. En route for Flogny.

150

To Ludovic Halévy

3 October 90
Flogny, Friday evening.

One needs to have been sad and serious for a long time to enjoy oneself so much. It is useless to be horrified at having such emotions. Our coachman is carrying the horse in his arms. The forelegs might betray us—42 leagues done with a real wisdom of the hand.

151

To Ludovic Halévy

4 October 90
Tanlay (Yonne), Saturday morning

Always get off at Dumas, innkeeper in the harbour, where we had lunch.

If I was the lunatic who thought of this journey, Bartholomé is the wise man who will finish by carrying it through.

18 litres of oats a day, is it enough? Your turn now, write to the Jeanniots at Diénay.

M. Jeanniot at Diénay par Is-sur-Tille (Côte-d'Or).

152

To Ludovic Halévy

5 October 1890
Aignay-le-Duc. Midday, Sunday.

Always to the minute. Not possible! We have just found at Copain where we are lunching some incredible gherkins. It is garden in vinegar. The Seine is there in which our horse has had a leg bath. There is only one country, it is ours, Monsieur.

153

To Ludovic Halévy

Molay (Côte-d'Or). 6 Oct. 90
Monday morning, 12.30

Go, learn a little geography, thanks to us. Almost arrived, seeing that we are only 11 kilometres from Diénay, we tell you, that the real traveller is the man who never arrives.

154

To Ludovic Halévy

7 Oct. 90 Diénay
Tuesday evening.

Arrived here at 4.30, a quarter of an hour too early for the manifestation. At the insistence of a person sent to meet us, we waited for the three strokes. Then a real policeman (Jeanniot) on horseback came and demanded our papers. A sub-prefect in uniform (Couturier) advanced with a dish and two keys and a speech, that the ladies interrupted by lancing, as from a cannon, the flowers of honour. General ecstasy, joy everywhere, a joy of excellent hearts.—Received your letter this morning.

Jeanniot, in his Souvenirs de Degas (*La Revue Universelle no. 11, Nov. 1st, 1933) gives the following details about the arrival of the two travellers: 'We were warned of the exact time at which the white horse was to appear on the road. All our friends were there, the young girls with their baskets of flowers, Edmond Couturier, as an inspector carrying the keys of the village on a silver dish. I myself, as a policeman, represented the public services. When the moment came the young girls advanced with their flowers, with which they covered the horse and the travellers. The keys were offered to Degas who was very touched by it. Our little band, escorting the carriage, entered the village slowly, with all the dignity worthy of the occasion.*

From 7 to 12 October Degas and Bartholomé stayed with M. and Mme Jeanniot at Diénay.

155

TO DURAND-RUEL

DARCEY (CÔTE-D'OR),
10 Oct. 1890.

DEAR MONSIEUR DURAND-RUEL,

I shall not be in Paris before Saturday or Sunday week. About Tuesday or Wednesday my maid, Zoé Clozier, will go to you. I should like you to give her 200 for which I shall bring you a repayment in objects

161

done by my hand. Poor Brown appears to want to resuscitate. I shall tell you how I am here in the serious moment of the 15.

Kind regards,

DEGAS

156

TO LUDOVIC HALÉVY

SAINT-SEINE-L'ABBAYE.
13 Oct. 90, Monday.

The journey was resumed yesterday at 3 o'clock. Follow on the map, from Diénay to Saint-Seine via Villecomte, where the two carriages, the one drawn by a donkey, with the families Jeanniot and Couturier, left us; via Francheville, Vornot, Prairay. First danger after Prairay, there was a sunset like in pictures; the outline of a calvary almost knocked us over.

157

TO LUDOVIC HALÉVY[1]

13 October 90.
Darcey, at Mme Bergeret.
Monday evening, 8.30.

Still unwell (did I tell you?) in spite of bismuth and doses of laudanum. Bartholomé, his hand swollen from a sting, swathed in antiseptic bandages, drives with his left

[1] From now on the letters are once again addressed in Degas' writing.

162

hand. Nothing can stop the carriage from crossing Saint-Seine (follow on the map, I beg of you, or I shall say nothing more), Bligny-le-Sec, Verrey, Gissey.

You do not possess, as Mme Bergeret does, two framed lithographs.

1st. Temple of Memories.

Chronology of famous women of the whole world,—from the creation down to our days.

2nd. Pantheon of the principal great men of the world.

158

To Ludovic Halévy

14 October 90.
Montbard. Tuesday, 2 o'clock

From Darcey via the Laumes, Marmagne, we follow the path.

Here is the country of Buffon. Essential to drop this truth into the letter box of the Academy: his *Histoire Naturelle* it is the funeral orations of the animals.

En route for Nuits. For the traveller the beat of the horses hoofs is sweeter than a woman's footstep.

159

To Manzi

14 October *1890*.
Montbard (Côte-d'Or). Tuesday.

Be prepared, we are returning, we are counting on meeting you on Saturday in check trousers and à la

163

Hussar, on horse or on foot, on the road from Montereau to Melun.

We have to be at Melun Saturday the 18, Hotel du Grand Monarque about 6 o'clock in the evening. To this warning, which you will receive to-morrow, you can reply Poste Restante at Sens, where we shall be Friday lunch-time.

See you soon,

DEGAS

160

TO LUDOVIC HALÉVY

Undated

The billiard table is the piano of the cafés (Bartholomé).

This man's right hand is in such a state that it ignores what his left hand is doing, which, alone, is mistress of the adventure.

The horse has never been fed like this; instead of weakening it is putting on weight. Moreover, I defy anyone to deny it, he knows that he is regaining Paris, he knows the direction without a map.

161

TO LUDOVIC HALÉVY

15 October 90.
Tonnerre. Wednesday 12.30.

You will reproach me for not having invited you to lunch at the Lion d'Or? One does not eat like that, once

164

one is a member of the Academy you will tell me—with one hand, the right one, I am writing to you, with the other I am eating a dish in which things are happening that chicken and veal can produce only here.—Bartholomé's right hand is eating grapes. We are living. Here is the cheese, it is as it should be.

The effect of the food on the horse is much more precise. It is a timepiece. From the terrace of the tilbury one ses under his tail, and according to the colour and quantity of what comes, we know what we have to know.— How does he know geography? He knows it. Do not tell me that the population of Yonne is decreasing, I shall not believe it.

I am re-immersing a biscuit into some white wine, and you will see us again after 182 kilometres, that is to say Monday, for lunch. There I shall eat no more.

162

TO LUDOVIC HALÉVY

16 October 90.
Saint-Florentin, 16 Oct midday.

Rain all night, but we were in bed. This morning the wind rises, chases away the clouds and drives us here in dryness. People clean their windows a lot in the province and they see nothing through these windows. That is what the man with the terrible left hand says. If we arrive in Paris without leaving the animal on his bad knees, you can say that he is some coachman.

165

163

To Ludovic Halévy

17 October 90.

Sens, midday.—Left Cerisiers at 7

The cold and the wind are increasing, we dined beneath the same sign at Mr. Tresse. Everyone has understood us; impossible to be commercial travellers. And yet the fat man, monk without orders, drinks white wine in an alarming manner. Wire from Forain, who is to meet us between Sens and Melun on a tricycle. How can a man of my age find himself in such an exalted position and not enjoy himself as we are doing.

164

To Ludovic Halévy

17 October 1890
Sens.

Telegram from Manzi: 'Shall be on road Melun to Montereau Saturday. Affectionately.' Go on, do something. Be less Montgeron, more Sénart. Be at Melun, be at The Grand Monarque, with a raincoat. They are harnessing M. Plumer (read Plumaire), our horse.

Do you want a fact, here it is: a thing, that costs more than women, is property.

Almost continuously walking pace.

En route to go and sleep at Mathé at Villeneuve-la-Guyard. To-morrow we are lunching at Montereau, sleeping at Melun. To-morrow, to-morrow, one should die in Sénart!

166

At Diénay we led a mondaine life, we dressed for dinner at M. Lemoine's, a man of 45 years, twice a widower, who, it appears, married at Reims, as a notary, who spent 800.000 francs on a property after the style of Enghien (formerly of Grandjean, Mme Jeanniot is from Grandjean).

165

To Ludovic Halévy

18 October 1890.
Melun, Saturday 7.30.

No Forain, but Manzi. At 10 kilometres from Melun a coupé advanced upon us. I had my revolver in my hand; it was Manzi, I did not fire. I must tell you that I am on watch and am always eager for danger. Arrival of the velocipedists at table. The wise B.[1] says that the hotels will find the income from the stage coach in the bicycle. Already we eat no more here.

166

To Ludovic Halévy

18 October 90.
Melun, 9.30.

One does not give Brie like that to Parisians! said Forain to the waiter. He arrived on his tricycle in a Garibaldian get up, he speaks of the destiny of speed—He is on his feet and speaking with a piece in his mouth.

Look after yourself, seeing that you are not here.

[1] Bartholomé.

167

167

To Ludovic Halévy

19 October 90.
Montgeron, Hotel de la Chasse.

Already the four assassins are waiting for their fried eggs. Soon each will be at home. We should have liked to find you here in good health and hurl ourselves at your table—we were rather quick from Melun, it seems to me. The coachman B. has a very bad hand. It is time he left the whip for a poultice. To-morrow.

168

To de Valernes[1]

Tuesday, *1890*

My dear Friend,

M. de Saint-Paulet came to urge me on your behalf to take the road for Carpentras. I shall go straight there, I shall go on to Geneva afterwards. You know that I have not stirred at all from Paris, glued to pictures that I do not finish.

And now your friend Morel has left and you must miss him many a time. So I shall see the good Salla again and the handsome Liébastres, and smell the scent of caramels.

It will be less cold than here, the cold arrived very bitter all at once.

It is probable that you will see me arriving Sunday or Monday. Moreover I shall send you one of those telegrams that astonish you so much.

Your old friend,
Degas

[1] Painter, friend of Degas. See annotations, p. 267.

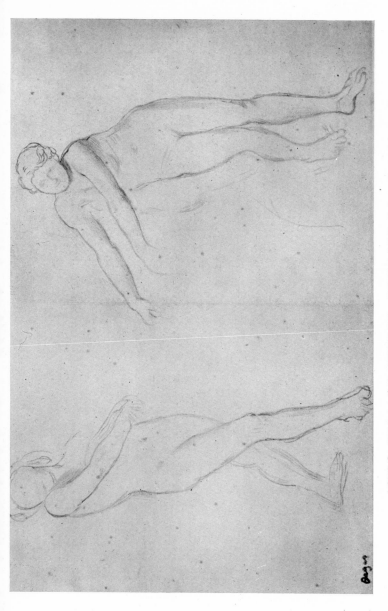

20. TWO FEMALE NUDES, STUDIES FOR DANCERS

21. BALLET DANCER

To De Valernes

Sunday. *1890*

Why no news from you, my old comrade?

The fine weather is coming at last, you will pick up a little, go out on the arm of M. de Saint-Paulet, leave your grotto for a while.

I was still waiting for a letter from M. Milon about the du Laurent family. I am afraid that his silence hides a little irritation.

On leaving you I went to spend the night at Lyon and early in the morning I left again for Geneva.

I saw the sculptor Lenoir[1] twice in the matter of your young marble cutter, and I have nothing to add to what I told you at your house. It is impossible to promise anything to a man of whose work one has seen nothing and of whom one knows only of one quality, that of being accustomed to the unique texture of the material, without any knowledge of the execution, with scarcely any studies of the nude. It is essential for this boy to get accustomed to the idea of risking all by going to Paris.

You will have received or you will receive the photographs of Bartholomé, who has retained a real impression of you. My regards to Madame Henriette and a handclasp for her.

I embrace you, my old friend; towards September you will see me at Carpentras, back from Cauterets.

Ask young de Saint-Paulet to present my respects to his mother, whom I must have offended. My regards to Mrs Milon, Salla.

DEGAS

[1] Alfred Lenoir, sculptor, 1850–1920.

To De Valernes

Paris, 26 Oct *1890*

I have been thinking constantly of you with the most affectionate feeling and I did not write to you, my dear de Valernes.

Your beautiful letter came to me in a little village, called Diénay in the Côte-d'Or, where we were, Bartholomé and I, led by the following adventure:

After Geneva, on leaving you, I met the said faithful friend at Dijon, from where we went to the said Diénay to see the Jeanniots, who live there for a third of the year, and after having left them and once back again in Paris, the memory of the pleasure of this spot and the desire to get to know a little better the admirable burgundy, brought me to such a pitch of travelling excitement that I persuaded my good comrade to share my folly.

And this folly now classified by us and by the others as an act of particular wisdom, could only be appeased by the hiring of a tilbury and a white horse, and by traversing in 20 days, 5 of which were days of rest at Diénay, more than 600 kilometres, that is 150 leagues.

When the fine season returns, we will start again with another horse (he is too weak in the forelegs), the same type of carriage and we will perhaps go as far as the rue Sadolet[1] to stir your old heart again, see your philosopher's house again, your museum, your room for drawing, allow you to get to know Bartholomé to whom I so often speak of you, of your energetic and tender life. All this will

[1] At Carpentras, where de Valernes lived.

alarm you. But you will not have the courage to tell me, that you are afraid. We shall leave or we shall not leave the animal at the Hotel de l'Univers and we shall drag you with us to Avignon, to see your Sainte Thérèse (she is in the museum, is she not?) to talk of Delacroix and of everything that can (it is art that we have the duty to practise) bewitch truth, give her the appearance of madness.

I see again you and your little studio, where I gave the impression of looking too quickly. I see it again, as if it were in front of me.

I can even tell you, that this survey has added almost nothing more distinct, for I had forgotten nothing and I found again your two phases of living (less divided than you think and than I, too, used to think). You have always been the same man, my old friend. Always there has persisted in you that streak of delightful romanticism, which adorns and colours truth, gives her that air of madness, as I have just told you, which does good.

Here I must ask your pardon for a thing which often comes up in your conversation and more often still in your thoughts: it is to have been during our long relationship to art, or to have seemed to be *hard* with you.

I have been unusually so with myself, you must be fully aware of this seeing that you were constrained to reproach me with it and to be surprised that I had so little confidence in myself.

I was or I seemed to be hard with everyone through a sort of passion for brutality, which came from my uncertainty and my bad humour. I felt myself so badly made, so badly equipped, so weak, whereas it seemed to me, that my calculations on art were so right. I brooded against the whole world and against myself. I ask your pardon sincerely if, beneath the pretext of this damned art, I have wounded your very intelligent and fine mind, perhaps even your heart.

That picture of the *Malade*[1] of which I can visualize not only the effect and the ensemble and the general air of simple unhappiness, but each stroke of the brush and the execution (as it were à la Duranty[2]), is a beautiful picture. The composition of the two Arlesian women, the way they are grouped, is delicious.

I found in you again the same vigorous mind, the same vigorous and steady hand, and I envy you your eyes which will enable you to see everything until the last day. Mine will not give me this joy; I can scarcely read the papers a little and in the morning, when I reach my studio, if I have been stupid enough to linger somewhat over the deciphering, I can no longer get down to work.

Remember that you must count on me when the moment comes. Write to me.

I embrace you,

DEGAS

My regards to Monsieur Liébrastes and also to the charming Salla.

171

To BARTHOLOMÉ

Carcassone, Place aux Herbes
In a café, of course at 10.30
Thursday 4 September.

I insist on writing to you in this place and in front of the market shaded by beautiful plane trees.

[1] Now in the museum at Carpentras under the title *La Convalescente*.
[2] See annotations, p 262.

172

Ministransque potantibus umbram platanus . . .

And I am drinking anisette and water.

I have come down from the city (Viollet le Duc) and I am waiting for 11 o'clock for the lunch at the hotel Bernard, in this café, on the fringe of this café. Yesterday I left Pau at 1 o'clock, and by pure chance made the journey as far as Lourdes with the chevalier Haase (sic) and the vicomte de Borelli. I was to have gone without stopping to sleep at Carcassonne, but about 6.30 at Toulouse I was too hungry, I stopped there because I knew that at the hotel Tivolier, I should for 5 francs be able to dine and digest a fine southern cuisine. But I had to make the tour of Saint-Sernin several times during the night, to hang around in a café and at the station of Matabiau, to wait for 11 o'clock for the express from Bordeaux to Cette and till 1 o'clock to get no sleep at the hotel Bernard. This morning I should have got up at 7 o'clock, I could have gone down to the city by carriage and taken the 9.30 train for Cette.

I got up at 8 o'clock, something you have never done; at 1 o'clock I shall leave this place which does not displease me. It is a long way to go from Pau to Geneva, also what am I to tell you about our meeting at Dijon! It is obvious that if I do not get to Geneva to-morrow, Friday, in the evening I shall certainly be there Saturday morning. Two days at Geneva, 1 Terrasse Saint-Victor, will suffice for me. So we could meet Monday evening or Tuesday morning at Dijon. Take this date as an approximate basis. I shall wire you from Geneva for more concentration.

Off to lunch at Bernard, it is time.

Affectionately, DEGAS

173

To De Valernes

6 Dec. 91

You have guessed right, my old friend, I do not write on account of the fatigue of writing, and except for a few laconic words, my sister Marguerite[1] is the only one to receive from time to time letters from me.

I see worse than ever this winter, I do not even read the newspapers a little, it is Zoé, my maid, who reads to me during lunch. Whereas you, in your rue Sadolet in your solitude, have the joy of having your eyes.

Your friend M. le Marquis de Saint-Paulet came, nearly a month ago, to see me and speak at great length about you! I shall go on Wednesday (his at home day) to return his visit. He must have there the portrait you did of him and with which he is very pleased.

I have allowed time to slip by without thanking you for your present of the picture of the milliners, or rather the florists, which I remember perfectly, with a supple woman's hand and a romantic style that I can see from here. It is I who am at the moment doubly your debtor, first of all because of my promise, and secondly because of this nice present.—This summer for certain I shall go and see you and you may count on my not arriving with empty hands.

Ah! Sight! Sight! Sight!

My mind feels heavier than before in the studio and the difficulty of seeing makes me feel numb. And since man,

[1] Marguerite De Gas, Mme Fèvre, 1843–1895. Degas did several excellent portraits of her, one etching, drawings and two sketches (Louvre). He has also given her features to the two singers in *La Repetition de Chant* (Coll. Mme Bliss).

174

happily, does not measure his strength, I dream neverthe-less of enterprises; I am hoping to do a suite of lithographs, a first series on nude women at their toilet and a second one on nude dancers.[1] In this way one continues to the last day figuring things out. It is very fortunate that it should be so.

Will you have the courage to come to Paris one day? There will always be a *pied à terre* for you with your old friend. Desboutin,[2] still young at 70 years, thrones with his pipes at the entrance of a café, you will see him again with pleasure. And others too! Permit yourself this in-discretion and when I am at Carpentras during the holi-days I shall make a more serious attempt to carry you off.

Goodbye, my dear old comrade, your letters give me great pleasure, write to me seeing that you have the good fortune to be able to do so better than I.

Regards to M. Liébrastes and to that Vallot. I spoke of him to M. de Saint-Paulet, who told me about his adven-ture in the drawing of lots for money and his well-being. What would you like in the way of books or anything else, I am at your disposal.

See you soon,

DEGAS

[1] This refers to the series of lithographs obtained by transferring on stone, drawings done with greasy ink and touched up with litho-graphic chalk: *La Suivante démêlant des Cheveux, La Sortie du bain,* a second *Sortie du bain, Femme nue debout s'essuyant.* (Catalogue Delteil, no. 62–65.) Of the nude dancers Degas only engraved one plate, a soft ground. (Delteil, no. 31.)

[2] Marcellin Desboutin, 1823–1902, dramatist, painter and en-graver. He specialized in drypoint on copper and made several por-traits of Degas and of Count Lepic in this manner. Degas represented him several times, in *l'Absinthe* and in another painting together with Lepic (both in the Louvre), also in the litho Delteil, no. 55.

175

To Aglaüs Bouvenne

1891

MONSIEUR BOUVENNE,[1]

So you are the exhibitor of this little programme[2] of the concert at the Quai Malaquais.[3] It was with surprise and anger that I read your name on the catalogue. So you did not think that you lacked my consent. You were not, I very much fear, at the concert and it is not from there that you received the proof. It is more than probable that, over and above the copies ordered and paid for by M. Clemenceau who directed the fête, you had your copy printed. It was an excellent reason to keep it in a box, or not to take it out without my consent. I should not have given it to you, and the idea of being represented in this lithographic revue by this unique piece would have seemed like a joke to me.

I insist, on all occasions to appear, as far as possible, in the form and with the accessories that I like. I can scarcely compliment you on your strange *sans gêne*.

My friend M. Alexis Rouart, who is, I think, on the committee, did not think that he could exhibit an attempt by Mlle Cassatt without writing to her. She replied that she would permit it. You did not show the same consideration.

[1] Aglaüs Bouvenne, 1829–1903, bibliophile, archaeologist and engraver, who did famous exlibris for Hugo, Gautier, etc.
[2] For the soirée of the old pupils of the lycée de Nantes, for which Degas had drawn a lithographic illustration (Delteil, no. 58).
[3] At the general exhibition of lithography, 21 April 1891, no. 956 with the note, Coll. Bouvenne.

Be good enough to have the six lithographic stones, that the maison Lemercier lent me some years ago for some attempts, fetched from 37 rue Victor-Massé. Very fortunately there is nothing at all on them.

I have the honour, Monsieur, to salute you.

DEGAS

174

TO AGLAÜS BOUVENNE

On a visiting card, 1891

DEAR MONSIEUR BOUVENNE,

If the stone of my little programme has not been effaced, please be good enough to have ten copies printed.

See you soon,

DEGAS

175

TO LUDOVIC HALÉVY

1st Aug. 1891

Today I am going to Chatou and I have not written you what has been arranged, my dear friend. So you are not going to the station with your retinue. To-morrow I have an appointment at 5 o'clock with the oculist Landolt, who will not, I think, keep me late enough to prevent me from arriving at the Gare du Nord in time for the 6.25.

I am being sent once more to Cauterets and I am leaving on Thursday. Last Thursday dinner at Durand, given by Cheramy[1] where I made the acquaintance of Bertrand,[2]

[1] Lawyer, famous collector; he specialized in Delacroix.
[2] Co-director of the opera with Colonne.

177

the man who likes to tell how he was nominated without once having asked to be.

Assuredly you should be in the railways; never an accident with you; you would be the good brake, the true signal, the switch itself, precision. In this way there would be something of everything at the Academy!

Affectionately,

DEGAS

176

TO BARTHOLOMÉ

Express telegram, 1891.
Friday evening 11 o'clock

My brother informs me that there will be a Buddhist mess at the musée Guimet to-morrow, read by two Buddhist priests. If I do not go (I am expecting my surgeon at home) it is essential for you to go. You have relations with this church. The little goddess, who knows how to dance will be invoked. Do not miss that, both for your sake and mine. All the details to-morrow evening.

DEGAS

177

TO BARTHOLOMÉ

Undated

But no, my dear Bartholomé, I was not mortally bored. You did not, I imagine, expect Floral games. If the con-

178

versation was not as sweet as one might have wished, at least we looked at one another a lot, and admit that that is not always sad.

Voltaire said: the first one to compare a woman to a flower was a lover, the second was an imbecile . . . You know whom I compare to a flower and what name I deserve. Wednesday we shall continue the appreciation.

Affectionately,

DEGAS

178

TO DURAND-RUEL

Paris, Sept. 1891

DEAR MONSIEUR DURAND-RUEL,

I should be much obliged if you would kindly send 570 fr. today to M. Cheramy, advocate, 21 rue Saint-Augustin. It is for a rent of 550 and a few francs payable to the administrator. My eyes are finally getting a little weary and I am going to rest for a day or two.

See you soon,

DEGAS

179

TO BARTHOLOMÉ

Undated

My dear friend, will you come and eat a spiced chicken with our poet,[1] on Saturday? I should have liked to have

[1] Probably Stéphane Mallarmé.

179

you earlier, Thursday for example, and now at Stevens orders it will be necessary to hear and perhaps even listen to his violinist. I also warn you, that the poet is going to leave.

Yours very affectionately,

DEGAS

180

To Ludovic Halévy

September 91.

I am writing to you still to La Chesnaie, so that you may be forewarned before you leave these charming parts. To-morrow, Monday, having heard that La Cigalle[1] has been postponed, I am having M. and Mme Forain to dinner and I do not intend leaving them to go to M. Edmond de Rothschild. This is what the conventions of friendship demand.

Except for Friday, I am ready for the Cigalle. And even Friday, although dining at the Rouarts, I could still be game for it. Bartholomé is warned.

Dinner yesterday at Cavé. Mme Howland sad; Haas always simple and delightful; Cavé gone very thin all the same.

Affectionately,

DEGAS

[1] Comedy by Meilhac and Halévy.

180

181

TO MADAME LEROLLE

4 Feb. 1892.

Thank you, dear Madame. Even had you added a little malice I should still be grateful. I well deserve at my age to be told to love the orange blossom more.

Affectionately,

D.

182

TO DANIEL HALÉVY

Ménil Hubert, par Gacé
August 1892.

But, Daniel, I left on the 8th. Your letter, brought by your comrade, reached me here, follow me if you like maps, arriving at Carpentras to go via Grenoble, Chambery to Geneva and finally to Saint-James. All that will take me a good 10 days at least. So little chance of contemplating one another before the 1st September. Greetings to your family whose pen you are rapidly becoming, legible enough to give me pleasure.[1]

Yours affectionately,

DEGAS

Regarding the letter I am unable to tell you if Mlle Yoyo[2] brought it up or not, if she dared to speak to Zoé. We shall find out. So when shall we drape her as Iphigenia? Have you a Thoas ready?

[1] Ludovic Halévy's writing was very fine and difficult to read.
[2] Nickname of Mlle Lemoinne, sister-in-law of J. E. Blanche.

If you want to have an idea of the nature of my thoughts, take the chorus of Euryanthe and listen to me singing all day long, in falsetto: *When we seek the king himself* . . . *Hunter lost in the woods*, with the interrupted cadence . . . *in the woods*. It is beautiful, disquieting, airy, firm.

183

To Bartholomé

Tuesday, Ménil Hubert.
16 August 92

. . . I am off towards the end of the week, to go I know not where. I should like to go to Nantes, to see the portrait of Mme de Sennones (sic), or else head straight for Carpentras in spite of a thousand difficulties. I no longer know how to conduct myself. Others have the good fortune to be guided by their passions. Passions, I have none . . .

184

To De Valernes

Château de Ménil Hubert, par Gacé (Orne)
Thursday

From here I am going to make straight for you, my old friend, vary the journey a little in spite of the oppressive heat. I did not go to Cauterets. You gave me no further news of yourself, I am reduced to the long letter, dictated to your young pupil. When writing to M. Milon for the death of his wife, I was hoping for a word from him, in which he would tell me how you are. And now here is poor Mme de Saint-Paulet gone so quickly. M. de Saint-Paulet replied at once with a letter to the telegram I had sent him immediately on hearing the news.

In a week or so I shall knock with the knocker of the rue Sadolet at your repose and your resignation, my old comrade. It will be necessary once again to forgive my turbulence; I feel each time that I agitate you a little too much.

I embrace you very affectionately,

DEGAS

185

To Bartholomé

Saturday, 27 Aug. 92

Just imagine I am still here. And yet it is necessary for me to leave. I wanted to paint and I set about doing billiard interiors.[1] I thought I knew a little about perspective, I know nothing at all, I thought that one could replace it by a process of perpendiculars and horizontals, measure angles in space by means of good will alone. I dug myself into it . . .

186

To De Valernes

Wednesday evening.
1893.

My old comrade, my kidneys make me grumble a lot, except at you, who have the goodness to think more of

[1] This probably refers to the two paintings 2nd sale Degas, no. 25 and 37. (No. 37 is in the coll. M. Couriot.)

183

me than I do of you. Otherwise I am well and I am dreading a stay in my room, without work, without being able to read, staring into space. My sight too is changing, for the worse. I am pitying myself, so that you may know that you are not the only unhappy person.

With regard to writing, ah! my friends can scarcely count on me. Just imagine that to re-read, re-read what I write to you, would present such difficulty, even with the magnifying glass, that I should give it up after the first lines. And with it all I am cheerful, as you were able to ascertain yourself.

Towards the end of the year, you will see me arriving, my old friend, to rouse you for a moment.

I embrace you very affectionately,

DEGAS

Thank M. Milon.

187

TO DE VALERNES

Saturday

I could not understand, my old comrade, my old friend, why both M. de Saint-Paul and M. de Milon left me without any news of you. From M. Lopin's hand I learn that you are well and that you desire to see me. I, too, I wish to see you and to embrace you.

Wednesday, the 10 of this month, barring serious accidents, I shall leave and am counting on bursting in on you rue Sadolet on Thursday morning. A wire will confirm my departure. You will see me with a comparatively omin-

184

22. BALLET DANCER

23. BALLET DANCER

ous looking contraption over my eyes. They are trying to improve my sight by screening the right eye and only allowing the left one to see through a small slit. Things are fairly all right for getting around, but I cannot get accustomed to it for working.

See you soon,

DEGAS

188

TO BARTHOLOMÉ

Tuesday *1893*

Thank you, my dear friend, I am writing to young Blanche, that I shall definitely be at Grenoble on the 6th, that he should wait until then. By the way, he did not seem to want the people at the address that he gave, to know that he was receiving money.

So I shall be off on my own. Three pictures kept me here for three weeks. You do not mention Salle?[1] Did you go on with the bust? and my poor clay?

The moment I return I intend to pounce upon Mme Caron. You should reserve her a place now amongst your precious relics.

Departure fixed for Thursday; Friday, Saturday *en marche*. Arrival quietly on Sunday in the Carpentras that you regret knowing only in barest outline.

Affectionately,

DEGAS

Mlle Salle, dancer at the opera.

189

To Ludovic Halévy

Hotel Jungfrau, Interlaken.
Monday 31 Aug. 1893

If I did not stop 3 days at Diénay near Dijon, with the Jeanniots, I should be with you on Wednesday, my dear Halévy, I am leaving here at 4 o'clock to spend the night at Dijon, where the self same Bartholomé must finally land.

Your vegetable garden must be burned up. Impossible to take one step without being bathed in perspiration. I have scarcely left the side of the poor invalid and my heroic sister.[1] Women have goodness when we are no longer worth anything.

I shall go and see Rouart before the end of his holiday in the Queue.

What a lot of Germans here, and Frenchmen, ridiculous too. If I did not feel myself to be simplicity itself, as the inn keeper at Cauterets told me, I should be worried about the impression I make.

It is impossible for me to live far away from my studio and not to work. In a few days I shall be content.

Greetings to Louise and her sons.

Affectionately,

Degas

---

[1] Edmond Morbilli and his wife Therese, sister of Degas, who painted several portraits of the couple (Sale René de Gas 1927 no. 71 and Coll. Mlle Fèvre in Nice) and of Mme Morbilli alone (a pastel, coll. David Weill, an oil painting in the Louvre and two drawings formerly Coll. René de Gas).

186

190

TO JEANNIOT

Tuesday
Postmark Sept. 1893

The glue is too strong for me, handsome Capt'n and heavenly being—I have shoved it onto Bartholomé, who will write to you about it. The difficulty, the skill lies in the length of time the glue is immersed in cold water. It must absorb the necessary humidity. You say 'Meixmoron'[1] always incorrigible. Why not? Corot said he never did anything that bored him.

Affectionately,

DEGAS

191

TO MLLE DIHAU

Tuesday evening
Postmark: 1894

Yes, dear Mademoiselle, until Friday, although this day belongs to my friend Rouart. I have disengaged myself so as not to refuse you, for it is a very long time since last we saw each other.—Thank you, and all my friendship.

DEGAS

[1] Author of descriptive catalogues of engravings.

187

192

TO MLLE DIHAU

DEAR MADEMOISELLE,

Saturday I am engaged, I am going to dine at Auteuil. Forgive me. And believe in my sincere regrets; you know what pleasure I always have with my friends, the Dihaus.

Sincerely yours,   DEGAS

193

TO BARTHOLOMÉ

Friday
Postmark: March 1894

You still retain, my very dear friend, strength enough to be singularly obstinate in making a martyr of yourself.[1] I complained a lot at the Jeanniots, where I stayed after having left you in a deplorable condition, and this condition irritates and pains them as it does me. They are counting absolutely on seeing you at dinner with us to-morrow.—Remember that all alone one is never entirely self-sufficing.   DEGAS

194

TO LUDOVIC HALÉVY

3 October 94
Wednesday,

Here I am, recommender of an actress, my dear friend. A Creole who, under the name of Schampsonn, conceals

[1] Bartholomé was inconsolable after the death of his first wife.

188

that of a noble family of Guadeloupe, and who posed for me quite simply, wishes to be admitted to the Conservatoire for the examination of the 17th of this month. Zoé has just introduced her with horror while I was lunching. Bertrand, she knows Bertrand, boasted to her of your influence. All for tragedy it seems. Lessons from Guillemot and from Paul Mounet; she would like to get into Worms' class. If you had been in Paris I should have taken her to you, but I know my distance and what is fitting, and I shall never take her to Sucy.[1] Do you want to see her? Could you, when you leave the academy on Thursday, let her place herself somewhere on the way, where you pass, in front of the Bastille or in the station of Vincennes? She will come and fetch your answer 1.30 rue Ballu. Ah! ye Gods.

Greetings,

DEGAS

195

TO SUZANNE VALADON

Sunday
Postmark: July 94.

You must have taken your drawings away from the Champs de Mars, illustrious Valadon. So come and bring me mine to-morrow morning. Bartholomé will have written to you about a drawing he was terribly anxious to have, is he suited?

Sincerely yours,

DEGAS

[1] Sucy-en-Brie where Halévy had his country house.

189

196

TO SUZANNE VALADON

Thursday
Postmark: November 94

Terrible Maria, yesterday at Lebarc (sic) de Bouteville, I wanted to buy your excellent drawing, but he did not know the price. Come if you can to-morrow about 9.30 with your box, to see if you have nothing even better.

DEGAS

197

TO DURAND-RUEL

Undated

DEAR MONSIEUR DURAND-RUEL,

Always money. Can you send me 300 francs to-morrow, Monday (200 francs for a bill for Portier for 400 francs, of which I have half, and 100 francs for my living expenses?)

I am not leaving your articles.

Greetings,

DEGAS

Sunday.

198

TO ALEXIS ROUART

Undated

MY DEAR FRIEND,

I left you in the lurch yesterday evening. It is not entirely my fault. I was, as usual, a little late. My sister came to read me a letter from Naples and for a chat, and I saw there was no longer time to get to your place.

See you in a fortnight then. I am working a lot. Durand Ruel sells all my articles and asks me for more. I feel well.

Very affectionately,

DEGAS

Wednesday morning.

199

TO ALEXIS ROUART

Monday

MY DEAR ROUART,

You did well to write to me, I was going to go and dine with you to-morrow. A thousand good wishes for the travellers to Allevard. I should much like to see you about a matter of lithographs, which preoccupies me very much. Gosselin[1] sent his son to tell me that he had 93 Gavarni proofs before letters (those of Lessore). I have seen them, the majority are very fine, and I told Gosselin that I could not make up my mind before you had seen them. And then I only want to take them gradually. He asks 550 francs for the lot, and I cannot spend such a sum all in one. Try and look at them. Examine them well, to see if they really are all proofs before letters, if there are not any with concealed letters, etc.

It is an excellent bargain, which will send my collection soaring up. You for your part, have you found anything?

Terrible, terrible.

Regards,

DEGAS

[1] Print dealer, quai des Grands-Augustins.

191

200

TO ALEXIS ROUART

Undated

MY DEAR FRIEND,

I am not coming to dinner to-morrow. Halévy is starting his Tuesdays again and he made the whole band promise to be there for the re-opening.

I am classifying my stock at Delorière. Sunday next, could you come to luncheon with me and lead me afterwards to the Danvin?[1]

I see from the calendar that your next Tuesday will be the 8 March, which is rather far off.

Wednesday morning I left everything to look by daylight, with a magnifying glass, and for a long time at the magnificent Gavarnis that you gave me.

I am keeping a special box for pieces of this class and I put beside each one an ordinary print which doubles my delight in the extraordinary one.

Do you understand, eh?

DEGAS

201

TO ALEXIS ROUART

Tuesday.

MY DEAR ROUART,

It is six o'clock. I am too worn out with my cold and my aches and pains to go and dine with you, as I

[1] A painter (1802–1842).

192

wanted to do. So I am remaining in the warmth and climbing up to my room to eat some soup, look at my lithographs and go to bed, thinking of them and of you.

Greetings,

Degas

202

To Suzanne Valadon

Saturday
Postmark: March 95

And now to-morrow I must go to Passy, terrible Maria. Do not miss coming the next Sunday, if you can, with new drawings. Now that you are well, work hard.

Greetings,

Degas

203

To Suzanne Valadon

Postmark: 30 March 1895

You see, my poor Maria, that I am still unable to climb up to see you. Zandomeneghi and Portier gave me news of you. I should like to have some myself. Courage and take care.

Degas

204

To Suzanne Valadon

8 Jan.

I have been in bed and am late in answering, terrible Maria. And will it reach you, this little thank you for your

193

good wishes and your continued remembrance? Are you still rue Cortot?

Come and see me with drawings. I like seeing these bold and supple lines.

Happy New Year,

DEGAS

205

TO SUZANNE VALADON

Friday

At last, terrible Maria, I am replying to your good wishes. It is influenza, it is bronchitis etc. You for your part, are you up? Happy New Year and good drawings that you will come and show me.

Tell me what has become of the picture. If it has been retouched, I should like to know what has been done.

Your friend,

DEGAS

206

TO LUCIE DE GAS, MARQUISE GUERRERO

Mont-Dore, 18 Aug. 95.

MY DEAR LUCIE,

I should not object to knowing the state of my affairs in Naples. It is a long time since any account reached me from there. Why did you not see, that at least from year to year I receive my balance?

I am waiting with some impatience for this return to order.

194

I have been sent here on the mountain for treatment. I am fairly confident. My attacks of bronchitis have made me very vulnerable and force me to protect myself better for the winters.

Love to both of you.

Your cousin,

DEGAS

Paris, 23 rue Ballu.

207

TO DESIRE DIHAU

Monday, *1895*

MY DEAR DIHAU,

You had not forgotten my poor Achille.

Well it is all over with him. He returned only to die here, almost as soon as he got back to where he was born. —His wife insisted on a family funeral only. And so I am announcing his death to a few friends.

Your devoted

DEGAS

208

TO LUDOVIC HALÉVY

Monday, *29 September 95*

I can well believe that you did not expect me yesterday, my dear friend, seeing that I had not written. You see that in spite of this stinking heat and the full moon, I cannot leave this filthy studio, to which love of glory binds me.

195

One fine day I shall burst in on you, with my camera in my hand.

Greetings to Louise the developer.[1]

DEGAS

209

TO JULIE MANET[2]

Postmark: 20 Feb. 96.

MY DEAR JULIE,

Durand-Ruel is willing to lend the small room, that is all. Reply immediately. If you have the exhibition I shall order the screen. We shall be able to place about 300 things.[3]

Regards,

DEGAS

210

TO MADAME S. MAYER

Saturday, *April 96.*

MY POOR MADAME MAYER,[4]

I arrived too late to press your hand. The convoy left before the appointed time. The poor man could not

[1] Mme Halévy developed Degas' photographs.

[2] Daughter of Eugène Manet and niece of Edouard Manet, later Mme Ernest Rouart.

[3] Refers to the posthumous exhibition of the works of Berthe Morisot, Julie Manet's mother, which was being organised by Degas together with Manet and Rouart.

[4] Mme Salvador Mayer kept a shop with her husband. After his death she carried on alone. Her chief business was drawings and engravings of the eighteenth and nineteenth centuries. She was a great friend of Degas.

live like that, but all the same you must have received a terrible blow.

See you soon, dear Madame. You have my deepest sympathy.

DEGAS

211

TO HENRI ROUART

Monday
Postmark: 25 May 1896.

So here is your posterity on the march. You will be blessed, oh righteous man, in your children and your children's children. During my cold I am meditating on the state of celibacy, and a good three quarters of what I tell myself is sad. I embrace you.

212

TO SUZANNE VALADON

Postmark: Paris, 27 June 96.

How are you, my poor Maria? Do let me have news of you. Good health.

DEGAS

Friday.

213

TO LOUIS GANDERAX[1]

Thursday
Yes it is true, my dear Ganderax, I was surprised by this act of journalism.

[1] Literary critic, dramatist, collaborator and friend of Meilhac, later director of the *Revue de Paris*. This letter was found amongst Degas' papers; it was probably never sent.

197

You saw my impatience very clearly at Mme Straus at table, when you quoted me to your neighbour. You must not disturb me any more. The danger and the vexation of being honourably mentioned, I thought I was safe in that respect from you . . . you will cause a little embarrassment between us.

Greetings to the household,

DEGAS

214

TO ALEXIS ROUART

Paris, 28 July *1896*[1]

I do not understand, and your cook must have told you so from me, my dear friend, Sunday when you managed to ring on three floors without being let in by people, who were expecting you. We were expecting you, Zoé and I, and we should certainly have heard you if you had made a noise, either rung or knocked. However! Should I thank you for your affectionate letter? Why do you stroke a tiger?

Moreover, for lack of Bengal he is going to ravage the Mont-Dore.

From there, in 25 days time, I shall put forward a little scheme to you. I should like, once the treatment is finished, to go down to Montauban, by dint of pulling strings, get the keeper of the museum to show me the whole lot of Ingre's drawings. It will be a matter of several days, listing, classifying, etc. Do you feel like joining in this sport?

I shall give you my address once I am housed at Mont-Dore and you can reply to me there.

[1] The year in Rouart's writing, the notepaper headed: de Tasset et Lhote, Fabricants de couleurs fines. Rue Fontaine 31.

198

Your brother writes from Touraine that he will be in Paris on Friday and that he is expecting me to dinner.

I have not done badly as regards work, without much progress.

Everything is long for a blind man, who wants to pretend that he can see.

My regards to Mme Rouart and ever your

DEGAS

215

TO SUZANNE VALADON

Friday.

It is now nearly a month and I have not answered your good wishes for the New Year (*several words thickly erased*). I was confined to my room with I know not what.—When fancy takes you or you have the time to come to Paris do not fail to come and see me.—I have a small commission for you from one of my friends, Mr. Dumont, a painter.

You say there has been sickness at your house. Is it better?

Your old

DEGAS

216

TO BARTHOLOMÉ

Tuesday.
Postmark: Les Bains du Mont-Dore
12 Aug. 1897.

I shall give your regards to Talmeyr,[1] at 7 o'clock sharp during the inhalation. He will have a little time to spare

[1] Maurice Tallmeyr, a well-known journalist.

199

for me during the day, reading and anti-Semitic[1] conversation—at the table d'hote on my right sits M. Lévy! With regard to Montauban I am counting on going there towards the 20th or 22nd. In 18 days the Mont-Dore will release me.

I replied with a heap of nonsense to Jeanniot, the art critic. Bad weather, difficult days, I breathe badly with bad headaches. It is, so they tell me, the altitude. However . . .

DEGAS

217

TO BARTHOLOMÉ

Wednesday.
Postmark: Les Bains du Mont-Dore.
12 Aug. 1897

Talmeyr thanks you and thinks that what you say about him is just what he wants. He tells me that he has quite recently sent an article on *the end of the press* to the Figaro, with regard to the lotteries being taken up by the newspapers.

You make me think a lot of Adam[2] that I was forgetting. It will be necessary to go very far afield to find something ingenuous. I know well that you do not want to take Felix Faure for Adam and Mme Adam for Eve, nor Zandomeneghi for Cain, nor Raffaëlli for God Father.

---

[1] The Dreyfus affair had begun. Degas was violently anti-Dreyfus.
[2] Bartholomé was doing a sculptured group of Adam and Eve.

200

24. BALLET DANCER

D.L.

25. THE COIFFURE

218

TO BARTHOLOMÉ

Wednesday.
Postmark: Les Bains du Mont-Dore.
August 1897.

You immediately thought of the danger that Zandomeneghi is leading us into—After the Canovas, whom will he strike next? M. Sinserre[1] (sic), secretary to the Minister of the Interior, has promised me a letter to the prefect of Tarn to the effect, that Ingres is mine and yours too if you come. Your eyes, your lights I mean, I should like to count on them.

My sight is getting decidedly worse, and I am having some rather black thoughts about it.

DEGAS

219

TO LUDOVIC HALÉVY

Mont-Dore, 11 Aug. 1897
Hotel de la Poste.

The Reszkés always make me think of you. Either Mme de Mailly Reszké is here, and did not want to go to a dinner for men yesterday evening at my doctors, or else she is on their estate in Poland, or she has become Mlle de Goulaine again.

What a fine fortune! And the studs and the sallys at 5.000 francs.

[1] Olivier Sainsère, state councillor; amateur and art collector of great taste.

201

After my cure I am going to Montauban where there are some drawings by Ingres, which suits me. I dined at Mme Howlands, poor snob in exile with dog.

Write to me a little, you or Louise. I am sad though gay, or the contrary.

220

TO BARTHOLOMÉ

Friday, 13 August 1897.

. . . I am continuing to think of the Adam and curious to see what you say. Is it far or near? Is it a savage or an Italian? It is his ingenuousness, for which I cannot think of the form. I can feel all the same that you have a fancy to see again the drawings of Ingres for the *Golden Age*. But the *Golden Age* was a society. And in the isolation of Adam and Eve lay their beauty. Saturday or Tuesday of next week I shall be liberated and then en route immediately.

So leave the celluloid and once again take up your pen . . .

221

TO MADAME LUDOVIC HALÉVY

19 August 1897.

Thank you, my dear Louise, for your good wishes. Thank Daniel also for sending the Albert Dürer and for having blinded me a little in one eye.

Rouart tells me that, during his visit to Sucy, your academician insinuated, that he should deflect Guillaume[1]

---

[1] Guillaume, relative of Mme Rouart, director of the École de France in Rome, then of the École des Beaux Arts in Paris, member of the Académie Française.

202

from his project. Good heavens! Why does he not let the man arrive. It is the first time that an artist (if he is an artist?) presents himself as a writer (if he is a writer?).

And then the turning movement!

After the Academy, great Preservation, Lord High Superintendent at Chantilly. Let him go and be hanged there.

All the same, I shall certainly come and see you one day in your castle.

DEGAS

222

To Suzanne Valadon

Sunday
Postmark: 97.

Thank you for your good wishes, terrible Maria, all the more because I have need of them. They tell me I am still delicate and must beware of cold on the left side. It is necessary, in spite of the illness of your son,[1] for you to start bringing me again some wicked and supple drawings.

DEGAS

223

To M. Le Maire de Montauban

Grand Hotel du Midi
Montauban, August 16 1897.

MONSIEUR LE MAIRE,[2]

With reference to our interview, you wish me to write you a *résumé* of it. In view of the bad state of my eyes

---

[1] The painter Utrillo.

[2] This letter was found amongst Degas' papers, stained, partly burnt, unfinished and unsigned.

203

I am forced to be much briefer than with my tongue. So I would ask you to put forward and if necessary to support my request to the committee, which is to make an exchange of photographs with the Ingres museum. The museum possesses some drawings relating to pictures by Ingres, that I have the good fortune to own. I shall have photographs made in Paris of what I have, and the museum will permit me to photograph what it has of relevance. I add that the reproductions that I am offering are non-edited . . .

224

TO SUZANNE VALADON

Tuesday.

I heard from Zandomeneghi, my poor Maria, that after your son you yourself had been very ill. I am writing to remind you again, that once you are up and about you must, seeing that your livelihood is now assured, think of nothing but work, of utilizing the rare talent, that I am proud to see in you; these terrible drawings, I should like to see some again. One must have more pride.

DEGAS

225

TO MADAME LUDOVIC HALÉVY

Sunday evening
15 November 97

It is not the Academy, it is a regimen to which I am now condemned and which prevents me from being seen.

204

Adhesions of the pleura to the lungs, that is my weakness, and I cannot go out into the street or loiter there and in the evenings, very nearly every evening, I listen to Zoé who falls asleep whilst reading to me; and the iodized cotton-wool scratches.

Thursday I am hoping to go and have dinner with you, if the doctor whom I shall see to-morrow or the day after, does not tighten up my incarceration. There you are!

I have a deal of bother as a manager.

How relationships change, how worthless one becomes, how one is no longer as one used to be.

Greetings.

DEGAS

226

TO HENRI ROUART

December 1897.

I was inconsolable, my dear friend, to know that you had been and gone. Your letter told me that you would come and see me, but never did I dream that it would be in the afternoon. For you there is no commission, no work, no anything that I would not leave for the pleasure of seeing you, do you hear, my old friend.

227

TO HENRY LEROLLE

18 December 1897
Saturday

But Thursday I am booked at Halévy's, my dear Lerolle, and you must excuse me.

205

It is in vain that I repeat to myself every morning, tell myself again, that one must draw from the bottom upwards, begin with the feet, that the form is far better drawn upwards than downwards, mechanically I begin with the head.

Greetings,

DEGAS

228

TO HENRI ROUART

Monday evening
Postmark: 7 January 1898

Dear friend, I should very much like Adrian to bring me back the drawing of Ingres to-morrow morning, which I was unable to go and fetch. If you add your report as an expert on quality and price, you would help me a lot. You understand it!

Greetings

DEGAS

229

TO SUZANNE VALADON

Saturday.
Postmark: Jan. 98

I found your good wishes, terrible Maria, on my return from Bartholomé who read us yours at table where they were brought up to him. I am not too bad except for the entrails, and often stay indoors. You will give me pleasure and not disturb me as you fear if you come one day, at the end of the day, above all with a box of beautiful drawings.

DEGAS

230

To Durand-Ruel

Postmark: 1898

Do not deprive me of the little copy of Ingres, do not affront me and grieve me thus. I really need it.

I shall go and look at it again during the day. It is a little soft, but I like that. I thought about it all night.

Greetings,

DEGAS

231

To Edouard?
Probably the Marquis Guerrero, husband of Lucie de Gas

1898

MY DEAR EDOUARD,

It is not possible to receive a more cruel blow than you have just had. I have seen similar blows around me and judging by the sight of the poor parents I consider them to be terrible. An old bachelor like myself can have known nothing of the joys and sorrows of a family—so they say.

I am still intending to go to Naples to visit such of my family as are still there. You should urge me a little for I am 65 years old.

Writing is a fatigue that I avoid with my unfortunate eyes, which will soon leave me. I work with the greatest difficulty, and that is the one joy I have.

Apart from the terrible news, your letter gave me pleasure. I do not like bickering and I compliment you on not liking it any more than I do.

I embrace Lucie and press your hand affectionately.

Your cousin,

DEGAS

Attached a receipt for you to keep.

232

TO JEANNIOT

Thursday.
1898

Your good letter exudes joy, my dear friend. To think of Madeleine the mother of a lovely little girl. I never thought after two years that she would take this step. It is two years, I believe, since she married, is it not?

And then Marcelle gives us back the contact that we were losing a little, my old and dear comrade, of whom I never think without a *certain* affection.

DEGAS

233

TO JEANNIOT

Friday
Postmark: 19 March 98.

MY DEAR FRIEND,

Now here is Bartholomé, who only just missed killing himself. The bicycle, of course. Go and see him. I have just left. He is in a pretty sad state whatever he says.

DEGAS

234

To Henri Rouart

Thursday morning.

My dear friend, give me your advice. There is a similar picture, a little bigger I fancy, at Montpellier, at the museum, legacy Bruyas. Send the thing back to me by the porter with your good diagnosis.

235

To Henri Rouart

Thursday morning.
Postmark: 30 June 1898

Try to find a moment, my dear friend, to go to Bernheim to examine three sketches of flowers by Delacroix, so that we can discuss them to-morrow at your place.

Greetings.

There are also two ancient Corots to verify.

236

To Henri Rouart

Monday—Hotel de la Poste
Mont-Dore.
Postmark: 30 June.

I am replying to your good letter to the Queue, my dear friend. You must have got back there from the Touraine. What with the treatment, the sweating, the headaches

209

(good sign that it is effective) one forgets here a little of one's life. In a word one vegetates fairly agreeably, because one knows that it will end.

In the evenings I digest and take photographs in the twilight. Good health. Beware of the sport of the countryside. Greetings.

237

TO HENRI ROUART

Saint-Valery-sur Somme.[1]
Monday.
Undated (*Postmark:* 22 August 1898)

Not a word to tell you, unless it is that, provided the wind blows from inland, it is as hot as at the Queue, my dear friend. I left like a whirlwind for here, instead of for Mont-Dore. Greetings to everyone. There are no other ideas to express.

238

TO ALEXIS ROUART

Saint-Valery-sur-Somme.
Postmark: September 98.

Here your letter found me, my dear friend. Were it not for landscapes[2] that I am determined to try, I should have

[1] At this period of his life Degas was wont to pay several visits to his friend the painter Bracquaval; whilst there he drew and painted several landscapes. In his studio, in boxes were found enlargements of photographs of the surroundings of Saint-Valery, which he had certainly developed himself and which he used for his landscapes, some of them bearing a striking resemblance to the photographs.

[2] Several landscapes in oils, notably streets and entries to villages, which were sold at the 3rd sale of Degas' studio in April 1919.

left. My brother had to go back to his paper on the 1st, and the landscape(!) kept me here a few days longer.

Your brother, will he believe this?

Have you tried flowers with ordinary plates or extra steel faced?

Difficulty, there is nothing but that. One does not speak of *affaires*,[1] so as not to cry with rage.

Greetings to Mme Rouart and to yourself.

DEGAS

239

TO ALEXIS ROUART[2]

Sunday (Undated).

You thought of your old friend all the same on your ramble. Thank you for your good letter, my dear Alexis. —Instead of rambles I have just spent Tuesday, Wednesday and Thursday at St. Valéry, and the fancy has taken me to return there towards the 15th of this month. Is it the urge to draw a corner for a picture or to eat cooked endive salad and French beans, which all of a sudden appealed to my heated entrails?

I am also impatient for the family Rouart to be back in Paris, because I am alone and abandoned. That Madeleine, I could spend whole days talking to her; what a particular (sic). Your father cannot be too bad, seeing that he sent Adrian to fetch the colours from Delphines.

Regards to the poor little woman, Mother of Madeleine and also to Madeleine's father.

Greetings,

DEGAS

[1] The Dreyfus affair.   [2] Son of Henri Rouart.

211

240

To X . . .

Paris 26 March 99.

MONSIEUR,

I do not wish to exhibit and am taking the precaution of replying to your second invitation so that the *sans gêne* of last year is not repeated. I thought that my silence would be enough and that by not accepting in writing I was quite simply refusing.

So I beg you, Monsieur, not to think that you have any claim on my independence, to refuse all offers of loans by dealer or amateur, and to permit me to believe that this international exhibition is an exhibition like the Champs de Mars or the Aquarellistes here, or any other one and not an agency.

I should have thought that our president, my old friend Whistler, would have defended my rights and not have permitted such a lack of consideration towards me. Perhaps he did not think of it.

Please accept, Monsieur, my respects.

DEGAS

It is understood that what I am writing to you must be passed on to every member of your committee or council.

241

To JOSEPH DURAND-RUEL

Paris, 2 Aug. 1899.

DEAR MONSIEUR,

So your father is not coming back? They are pestering me about Berthe Morisot.

212

I wish you would have the goodness to send me a little money to-morrow. 500 francs. Here I am short.

Many thanks,

Degas

242

To Suzanne Valadon

Postmark: 3rd January 00, Paris.

I dined with Bartholomé yesterday evening, my dear Maria, and we remarked that every year on the same date we received a letter from Maria wishing us all the best, excepting the pleasure of seeing her drawings and of seeing her herself. And then, do you still draw, excellent artist?

Degas

243

To Hortense Valpinçon

8 January

How are you, my dear Hortense? You tell me nothing. And yet you are not one of those people who are exempt from all ills, in the Deux-Sèvres or elsewhere.

I was not too bad and felt myself young, but that has just ended badly. It is now 8 days that I see nothing and it is hard for me not to wander around a little outside after a day in the Studio.

And when I have not worked for a few hours, I feel guilty, stupid, unworthy.

213

Come back so that I can embrace you better than through the post.

Your old

DEGAS

244

TO LOUIS ROUART
At the Institut français d'Archéologie Orientale,
Le Caire (Egypte)

16 March 1900.

It is very late that I am answering your affectionate letter, my dear Redhead. I write so little, that I am losing the habit. And it is not due to lack of thinking of you, and of enjoyment at hearing your delightful letters, which are sometimes read to me. You are spending down there, some of the happiest years of your life. And if you wished to add to the tales of the Thousand and one Nights one tale on the joy of redheadedness, you would be doing something good.

With regard to brown, we have Ernest who, after having been shy and cold is becoming self-assured and warm. Wednesday towards 7.15, he arrived on foot with Julie to dine with Uncle Alexis, with such a married air that you would have rocked with laughter. 'Already,' I said to him. And Julie, who only opens her beak a little more, seemed just as much at her ease as he was. It is astounding how man and woman were made for each other, Mr. Prudhomme would say and I too.

They say you want to see your family again and your poor country. You will be here for the marriage, will you not?

214

These Boors will astonish us yet, as Kruger promised. Are they going to rise or perish? Lipmann shows no sign of any other feeling than what you know of him.

Write to me again. You gave me so much pleasure. I embrace you, my dear child.

DEGAS

245

TO TALMEYR

Postmark: 30 April 00

It is too long since last we saw each other. Come to dinner on Thursday, with Forain, Mme Potocka,[1] at 7.30, 37, rue Victor-Massé. No excuses allowed.

DEGAS

246

TO PAUL POUJAUD[2]

25 June 1900

MY DEAR POUJAUD,

Do come and have dinner with me next Wednesday. You will see some new things, above all a small Cuyp.

I am counting on you.

Greetings,

DEGAS

[1] Countess Potocka, née Pignatelli d'Aragon, who was famous for her beauty.
[2] Lawyer and amateur of art. See appendix p. 233.

247

To Henri Rouart, La Queue-en-Brie

8 August.

No, you do not see me at the Hotel de la Poste, seated beside Mlle Roger and her mother, tiny like a historic doll, leaning over, the better to hear the good that is being said of me. But know, that if you commit one single indiscretion either at La Queue or elsewhere, instantly this concert of praise will turn to malediction.

It is nasty, wind and rain.

And I cannot read and I can only think of my friends and of this damnable painting. A tear for me, nothing but that. Greetings to all.

Degas

248

To Alexis Rouart

17 Sept. 1900.

Yes, I shall go and have dinner with that excellent wise man on Wednesday. Delphine[1] says that the artists have invaded the Creuse. There were vipers there already.

Ever yours,

Degas

Monday.

[1] Mme Tasset. Tasset and Lhote were colour manufacturers. Degas spent many evenings with them enlarging his photographs.

26. BALLET DANCER

27. BALLET REHEARSAL

249

To Henri Rouart

Sunday

All the same, whatever trouble and difficulty I have in writing, I do not intend to leave you without an answer, my dear old friend. So he has passed away, the poor old wandering jew.[1] He will walk no more, and if one had been warned, one would certainly have walked a little behind him. What did he think since the revolting *affaire*?[2] What did he think of the embarrassment one felt, in spite of oneself, in his company? Did he ever say a word to you? What went on inside that old Israelitic head of his? Did he think only going back to the times when we were more or less unaware of his terrible race? We shall speak of it again when I see you again.

Wednesday I went to La Queue and I told them of a strange dream I had two days after hearing of his death at Tassets. Just imagine that I met him with a few more hairs on his head and that, as if I were awake, I had the presence of mind to stop myself just as I was going to say to him: 'Why X . . . I thought you were dead.'

So one keeps one's memory in a dream . . .

250

To Durand-Ruel

Paris, about 1900

My dear Durand-Ruel,

Please say, that this head is not to be varnished, the re-painted parts must dry for a long time.

[1] A mutual friend of Degas and Rouart.   [2] The Dreyfus affair.

217

We shall reckon this article at 1.200 francs if you please.

I have a cold and hardly ever go out. You would give me pleasure by sending me 660 francs to the studio where, rather late, I am keeping in the warmth. It is a canvas of the approved size, an old frame of about 30 years ago will fit. I did not find any in my store.

Sincerely yours,

DEGAS

251

TO SUZANNE VALADON

Sunday *1901*

Your letter always reaches me punctually, with its vigorous engraved lettering. It is your drawings that I no longer see. From time to time I look at your red chalk drawing in my dining room, which is still hanging there. And I always say: 'That she-devil of a Maria, what talent she has for that.' Why do you show me nothing more? I am getting on for sixty seven . . .

252

TO DURAND-RUEL

Paris 28 August 1901.

DEAR MONSIEUR DURAND-RUEL,

I wish you could manage to send me another few francs to-morrow, Saturday.

I should also like to show you a *Blanchisseuse* which I have succeeded in finishing. You will recognize her.

Greetings,

DEGAS

253

TO SUZANNE VALADON

Tuesday

Every year, terrible Maria, I see this clearly incised handwriting arriving. But I never see the author arriving, a box under her arm. And yet I am growing very old. Happy New Year.

DEGAS

254

TO ALEXIS ROUART

Monday.
September 1903.

Your wrote me a good letter the other day and I did not reply. I do not like writing, my dear friend, I only know how to talk, even when I do not know what to say.

One is still here in this studio after doing some wax figures. With no work, what a sad old age!

And your fishing? The papers are bringing a big angling competition. There are people who catch four or five fishes weighing no more than a pound in all, and they are mentioned and receive 50 francs.

Greetings to Mme Rouart.

I saw your brother the other day. He spoke to me again of Mme Brando[1] (sic).

See you soon,

DEGAS

[1] Mme Brandon, sister-in-law of Edouard Brandon the aquarellist, who was a friend of Degas.

255

TO BRACQUEMOND

Wednesday 30 December 1903.

The person who could give you news of me was I, my dear Braquemond, and who would have liked to have news of you. We must really try and see each other again before the end. Have you forgotten the monthly review[1] that we wished to launch in the old days?

DEGAS

256

TO HORTENSE VALPINÇON

Monday, 3 August *1904*.

MY DEAR HORTENSE,

This is what I should like to do in reply to your kind suggestion. I am writing to Henri that I am going to have a short stay at Ménil Hubert, by taking the train on Friday at 12.30 which will get me to Gacé about 7 o'clock, I shall be able to go and dine with you about 8 o'clock. If a different route seems better to them please ask him to write to me. If it is convenient please fetch me at Gacé. Thank you for your kind thought. Although I am not very well with my gastritis, I think I can permit myself this.

I embrace you. Greetings to Jacques.

Your old

DEGAS

Will you pass via Paris when you go to Normandy?

[1] *Le Jour et la Nuit.*

220

257

To Paul Poujaud

Monday *August 1904*.
37, rue Victor Masse.

My dear Poujaud,

I am addressing the wise traveller. Here is what it is about. My doctor, after the seven recurring attacks of gastric-intestinal influenza, prescribes a cure in the mountains, to get rid of the poison which has me in its grip. Give me an idea. Where should one go, without going as far as Switzerland, which bores me? The Pyrenees are far and hot, unless you know a cool corner there, not expensive. Not too much of a watering place. I was talking about it to Alexis yesterday at the Queue and he said at once: Go and see Poujaud. But he has already left. What do you say to the Jura? I need pure air. My tongue is still coated, my head hot and heavy, my morale low. Gastrology is a mental illness.

This note will perhaps reach you in your revelry. I am counting on still being here in eight days. I scarcely count on leaving here before the 10th.

Degas

258

To Durand-Ruel

Paris, 10 August 1904.

Dear Monsieur Durand-Ruel,

It is on you that I am still counting for the 3.500 francs that I must pay the man, to whom the little Brame had to sell his credit of mine, as I told you the other day. I am working like a galley slave, so as to be able to give you something soon. I am reflecting bitterly on the art, with which I managed to grow old without ever having found out how to earn money.

All the same, you will see some new things very far advanced.

Many thanks. Come Saturday at the end of the month with 4.000 francs (500 francs for me).

DEGAS

259

TO DURAND-RUEL

Pontarlier, 28 August 1904.

DEAR MONSIEUR DURAND-RUEL,

Be good enough to send me to-morrow morning, Thursday, 400 francs, half of which I must send at once to Naples. I have just received some new stamped papers that I am sending to you. I am very much annoyed.

DEGAS

260

TO DURAND-RUEL

Pontarlier, 1 Sept.

DEAR MONSIEUR DURAND-RUEL,

Be good enough to send me 200 francs here to Pontarlier, Poste Restante. I am counting on getting it on Saturday. This air cure is doing me a lot of good. I shall stay another ten days or so. See you soon.

DEGAS

261

To Alexis Rouart

Pontarlier, 7 September *1904*

It is raining, I am in a café. One thinks of one's friends when one is bored, one has no pleasure in oneself. I was waiting to reply to your good and long letter, my dear friend, until I was a little forced to do so by a damnable day. That is how one is, no worse than any other.

And so one left Paris at last, on the doctors orders, to sample the altitude. From Paris to Epinal, Gerardmer, La Schluchte (sic) passed to Alsace, Munster Turkeim (sic), Colmar, returned to France, Belfort, Besançon, Ornans, and finally stayed 15 days at Pontarlier from where I radiate a little. I shall return via Nancy, I shall have done more than the three weeks recommended. Without Grosjean the deputy, who kept me company a little, I should not have chosen this absinthe factory.

See you soon may be—I really need to see you again all of you, all of you Rouarts.

Greetings to your wife.

Your old friend,

Degas

262

To Alexis Rouart

Postmark: 27 Dec. 04.
Paris, rue Fontaine.

It is true, my dear friend, you put it well, you all are my family.

And so Sunday with pleasure.

Degas

223

263

To Henri Rouart

Saturday.
Postmark: 7 October 1905

Your brother writes me, that you have had a fresh attack of gout, poor unfortunate man. But you are not the only one. Come back soon, enough country.

Ever yours,

Degas

264

To Hortense Valpinçon

January *1906*

Every year we embrace from a distance, my dear Hortense, seeing that you love the country in the winter. I shall not tell you much with eyes as poor as mine.

Come back so that we can talk a little.

The news from Italy overwhelms me.[1] They write me nothing from over there, which means that we are not affected at our place. What a date this disaster will represent in history.

I embrace you.

Your old friend,

Degas

[1] An allusion to the eruption of Vesuvius in 1906.

224

265

TO DURAND-RUEL

Paris, 12 October 1906.

DEAR MONSIEUR DURAND-RUEL,

I am still counting on you for Monday, the damned rent (2.000). It will be necessary all the same to get down to painting. Many thanks.

DEGAS

266

TO JEAN ROUART

17 Jan. 1907.

Your father reminded me yesterday evening, my dear Jean, that I did not reply to your good letter. You cannot imagine to what a degree my sight, which still exists a little, keeps me from writing—it is pain, it is disgust, anger.—Will you be able to read me? I myself am incapable . . .

I came back from Naples a few weeks ago, family affairs. —One of these days I shall certainly do a tour in your part of the world.

I embrace you and wish you a happy New Year.

DEGAS

267

TO HORTENSE VALPINÇON

17 Jan. *1907*

With my poor eyes, my dear Hortense, I am losing the taste and the duty of answering. I let my good and faithful

225

friends send me such good wishes and I remain dumb and above all blind. Do come back here for a while so that I can embrace you, it is what I can do best.

I was in Naples at the end of October and did not get back to Paris until December, all that on family business, or rather on property because, as I told them over there, family is what divides us most. Come back so that I can embrace you a little.

Your old

DEGAS

268

TO ALEXIS ROUART

6 August *1907*

I am not worth very much as regards correspondence, my good friend.—My excuse might be that you were expecting it.

I am still here working. Here I am back again at drawing and pastel. I should like to succeed in finishing my articles. At all costs it must be done. Journeys do not tempt me any more.—At about 5 o'clock one dashes out into the surroundings. There is no lack of trams that take you to Charenton or elsewhere.

Sunday I am going with Saint-Maurice to see your brother who is gradually recovering. In the evening one returns to the great city.

I have pains in my kidney, which will not stop. And you, where are you with your pains? Write to me. You have a fine handwriting.

226

My good wishes to Mme Rouart.

Your old friend,

DEGAS

Chialiva son came to carry me off on behalf of his father in the Puys-de-Dôme.[1]

269

TO DURAND-RUEL

Postmark: 1908

DEAR MONSIEUR DURAND-RUEL,

As usual I am counting on you for the 15. Be good enough to reserve me 2.000 francs and to send them to me to-morrow, Tuesday.

I did not dare to speak of money yesterday in front of the model.

DEGAS

270

TO ALEXIS ROUART

21 August *1908*

Do not be angry with me, my dear friend, for replying so late to your good (sic). Soon one will be a blind man.

Where there are no fish one should not try to fish. And I, who want to do sculpture.

Good health to both of you,

DEGAS

[1] Jules Chialiva, the son of the Italian architect, painter and scientist, Luigi E. Chialiva, whom Degas had met in Rome about 1865. From him Degas had learnt the art of fixing pastels.

Instead of going to the Auvergne Degas visited Chialiva at Laon where he was doing some architectural drawings in the cathedral.

227

271

TO DURAND-RUEL

Undated

DEAR MONSIEUR DURAND-RUEL,

Here is a thing. You will guess the rest, the rest in the shortest possible delay.

Take care, I am going to raise my prices. Life is getting very short, and it takes too long to earn money.

Sincerely yours,

DEGAS

I shall gladly receive the samples this afternoon. Perhaps we shall both achieve wealth, at the moment when we no longer need it!—So let it be.

272

TO DANIEL HALÉVY[1]

Postmark: 17 June 1909.

MY DEAR DANIEL,

I cannot make a rendez-vous. All these days I am a little in the air.

Best wishes to your mother.

DEGAS

[1] We had asked Daniel Halévy to take us to see Degas being very anxious to make his acquaintance. Rendezvous had been made. In the meantime the famous ceramist Chaplet died and the funeral was fixed for the morning of our visit to Degas. He had been our friend of long standing so we asked Daniel Halévy to make our excuses to Degas and to arrange for another rendezvous; he only received the above answer and did not dare to insist. (M.G.).

To Alexis Rouart

Monsieur A. Rouart
Grand Hotel Bellevue
San Remo.

Postmark: Paris, rue Fontaine, 11. 3. 10.

Friday

No, my dear friend, I am no longer of these artists who race to the Italian frontier. One remains in the damp, facing the Bal Tabarin.[1] You will soon return to our waters.

I do not finish with my damned sculpture.

Greetings,

Degas

[1] Dance-hall opposite Degas' studio, rue Victor-Massé. Degas never entered it.

APPENDIX
Paul Poujaud, George Moore, Daniel Halévy

THREE LETTERS FROM PAUL POUJAUD
TO MARCEL GUÉRIN

Paul Poujaud, a lawyer, was known for his artistic culture and sure taste. He knew all the leading musicians and all the great painters of the period. His judgment and opinions carried great weight and his influence was considerable. He belonged to the type of 'Dilletante', was an excellent conversationalist and used to recount in the most vivid manner his memories of a whole life devoted to art. Unfortunately he never wrote anything down.

15 January 1933.

MY DEAR FRIEND,

Here are the notes you wanted on the portrait of Pagans.[1] My memories which go back forty years are very accurate. I had dined tête a tête with Degas. After the coffee he placed his hand on my shoulder, smiling and confident and made a sign for me to follow him. He took me into his room and showed me above the little iron bed the precious picture. 'You knew Pagans? It is his portrait and that of my father.' Then he left me alone. It was his manner of showing me his works. Through a sort of proud modesty he did not assist at the examination. It was in this manner that I saw *La Dispute*[2] before it was re-touched, and many other pictures retained or returned. After a few minutes he came into the room again and without saying a word, without a word from me, he

[1] See letter No. 49.
[2] Incorrectly called *Le Viol*. See next letter.

233

looked into my eyes. That was enough for him. He was always grateful for silent admiration.[1] I am certain that he did not show me the Pagans as a memory of his father whom I had never known, of whom he had never spoken to me, but as one of his finished works which he valued among the highest. . . . Later Degas told me that of the things he had, he liked three particularly; M. de Mornay's room, the pastel portrait of Mme Manet . . . and he did not name the third. I understood clearly that it was the Pagans. At the sale of the Degas collections I told Koechlin[2] and Leprieur[3] of Degas' predilection for the Delacroix and the Manet. They had the delightful idea of buying them. I should be very happy if the third favourite picture could join the two others. I am not shocked by the finish of the portrait. It is the mark of many beautiful works. I wish you may succeed.

Affectionate regards,

PAUL POUJAUD

20 Jan. 1933

MY DEAR FRIEND,

I am very pleased with the purchase of the Pagans by the 'Friends of the Louvre' and I congratulate you on it. It is you who found the picture and who have put it in its right place.

What date? I am very uncertain. Without much thought I suggested 1871 or 1872. The Pagans vogue in the

[1] He once said: 'With people, who understand, there is no need for words. One says: "Hm! He! Ha!" and all is said.'
[2] Then President of the National Museum Council.
[3] Then Keeper of Paintings at the Louvre.

234

Parisian studios and salons was, if I remember rightly, between 1871 and 1876. No confirmation whatever and with all reserve: I incline to 1872. One's memory can be deceptive with regard to a few years, I have often had proofs.

With friendly greetings

PAUL POUJAUD

11 July 1936.

MY DEAR FRIEND,

As you can imagine your letter stirred me deeply. It recalled to mind that unique work of Degas[1] . . .

Here is what I can tell you about the picture. I saw it for the first time in 1897. At that time, I have already told you, I often used to have lunch with Degas, tête a tête, the proper way to see him. After the morning's work he was a vivid conversationalist. I pity those who only saw Degas the grumbler. Moreover, a bad sign for them. After Zoë's good coffee, we looked for a long time at the new purchases, Monsieur Leblanc, M. de Mornay's room, Manet's pear . . . and then, if an old work of his had returned, he would place it in front of me on the floor against the wall and go out in his proud modesty, without saying a word. It was thus that he showed me the picture we are interested in. When he returned he smiled as he looked at me. 'You know my genre picture, don't you'— He never called it *Le Viol* to me. That title is not from his lips. It must have been invented by a literary man, a critic. I cannot say if it had been retouched when I saw it.

[1] The *Scéne d'Intèrieur*, also known as *la Querelle* or *la Dispute* and incorrectly as *le Viol* (Philadelphia Museum).

235

But I trembled when I remembered everything that he had spoilt with his retouchings. You will doubtless know now *Les Danseuses à la barre* came into the possession of Henri Rouart. He had bought an old pastel of Degas who was annoyed on seeing it at the Friday dinner. 'I forbade you to buy anything of mine!'—But on leaving he took the picture under his arm—'to look at it again in peace'. Poor Rouart knew that he would not see it again. A little later, Degas came back with another picture. 'Here, I spoilt your pastel, take this in its place'. It was the *Danseuses à la barre*, that Rouart, now warned, kept padlocked. But as regards the *Querelle*, I think that the re-touchings were very slight.—The date of the picture! I should place it before 1870—but quite indefinite.[1] . . .

I remember Degas often saying to me 'In our beginnings, Fantin, Whistler and I we were all on the same road, the road from Holland. Go and see at the exhibition in the Quai Malaquais a small picture, toilet scene by Fantin; we could have signed it, Whistler and I.'. . .

Yours sincerely,
PAUL POUJAUD

TWO LETTERS FROM GEORGE MOORE TO DANIEL HALÉVY

MY DEAR HALÉVY,

You tell me that it is to me that you send the first copy of the letters of Degas, it is a delicate flattery. I flatter myself that I deserve it, for I consider that no one is able to understand these letters as well as I can, not even

---

[1] Rather 1868 or 1869, so we believe.

236

their marvellous editor Daniel Halévy, who asks himself in the first place if Degas is a good letter writer, and to prove the affirmative quotes the first letter.[1] My dear friend, the first letter is a very good letter, but it is a conventional letter. It is a very good letter such as you or I or half a dozen other people could have written. It is exactly the letter we could have expected from a man who is far away and who feels bound to tell his friends what he thinks of the people of New Orleans or of the Argentine Republic—I have forgotten the country, it matters little. The book of Degas is the most marvellous collection of letters in literature because in the small letters Degas paints his own portrait. Wherever he goes he takes his studio with him. His difficulties with the printer, his money difficulties, the portraits which are not finished and which will not be paid until the day they are finished, the chasing after 5 franc pieces—what humiliation! The daily life of the man is related as Durer might have related his. Degas admired the Middle Ages, all his life he tried to equal Durer and he was unable to do so. Nobody can ever equal Durer. But what Degas did in his letters comes very near to Durer. All the intimacy of the Middle Ages lives again in these little letters for which you register such disdain. You will not like this remark but you wanted to know exactly what I think, and I am telling you. When he writes to your mother 'My dear Louise' it illuminates the full intimacy of this conversation with friends. And the familiar form of address to your father.

I am not speaking of these marvellous letters as well as I could have done, if I had written to you immediately or if I were to reopen the book and devote myself to them

[1] Our letter, No. 11.

237

for an hour or two. It is a book about which I could have written an excellent article. But this dictated letter will give you my point of view, and I think you will find that it is right. It throws light on the original nature of these letters—always written to a small circle of friends. Degas cannot leave Paris for one week or for one month without writing to some of them, and his studio is always with him—I repeat the phrase, on purpose. To put my meaning quite clearly, I should not speak of a 'collection of letters'. The letters of Degas are something of a diary, a little more and a little less than a diary. An admirable letter is the one in which he puts the printer in his place.[1] He finishes by an: 'I salute you'. In his style there is as it were a perfume of the fifteenth century, and yet he never once uses an archaic word, and from that one can understand that he was horrified by the neologisms of the Goncourt. I have read such a phrase of the Goncourts half a dozen times without succeeding in penetrating the meaning.

One single word in the book was unknown to me,[2] and when I looked it up in my dictionary, I saw that it was simply the good old word that I had known all my life, courge (pumpkin). Why did Degas not write 'courge'? A splendid word, a sonorous word, a roseate word, a word which has a history. Was it not from a 'courge' that the fairy fashioned Cinderella's coach? She did not fashion it out of a . . . I have forgotten the word and I want to forget it. For a moment it spoilt the book for me. The more I write of this letter the more I regret the excellent article that I could have written about those letters. Alas! it is lost for ever, for one or two reasons which I shall tell and then I shall stop.

[1] See letter, No. 173.   [2] 'Potiron' in letter, No. 93.

238

During the last three months, I have tried in vain to write a little story about nothing in particular. In vain did I set my heart on it, dig myself into it, persevere; I got nowhere. And this morning for the first time, whilst still in bed, I saw my story, I saw it from start to finish, written as it should be written. A story which abhors all naturalism, which requires to be written in the style of the fifteenth century. I do not mean the words but the general character.

Ever yours, my dear friend . . .

P.S.—You would do me a real service by writing, on a postcard as soon as possible, the correct spelling of Delisle in fifteenth century French—or, without specifying the exact time, in old French.

Bravo, I replied: and I must have expressed myself badly, or you must have understood me wrong, for I admire the letters of Degas exactly in the way you admire them. Whereupon a second letter:

MY DEAR HALÉVY,

It is a pleasure to write to an old friend about a book that one admires together. But I am sorry that you did not feel that my first lines were written in a spirit of affectionate raillery. Could it be otherwise in view of the tact and exquisite sympathy with which your edition was done? Your notes, I am convinced, are exactly the ones that Degas would have approved—they elucidate the text.

I have not yet read quite all the letters, a few pages remain, but I hasten to tell you (it is always a pleasure to communicate one's thoughts even if it serves no purpose) of one thing that struck me and which most certainly struck you, and that is that these letters reveal the real Degas. For a reason unknown to himself, Degas—never did a more sensitive human nature breathe beneath our skies—took devilish pains to persuade the world that he was an old bear incapable of finding a friendly word for anyone. The exact opposite is the truth. Nobody could ever write a life of Degas. These letters are his autobiography; even they do not give everything, and a first class writer, Balzac for example, could write some pages about a man who cannot resist the temptation of adorning himself out of coquetterie, with the mask of an old bear. What an innocent perversity! Another thing: no one but Jean Jacques could have given a portrait of such intensity. But Jean Jacques, in his Confessions, knows the effect of each line on his reader. Pen in hand Degas was the least self-conscious writer I ever remember. And by a long way. But take away his pen, give him a pencil and let him draw. Instantly he is a different man, his look changes, radically: the ambition of the Goncourt brothers would have been to write a book of a similar quality to the letters of Degas, but they did the exact opposite. And for Degas it was only necessary to lay aside his pencil to rid himself of all moral or artistic intentions.

One of the passages that delighted and astonished me most is the journey by carriage. Journey, is that the right word? In French you have 'randonnée', it is perhaps the word I need. I should like to be able to put down in black and white my admiration for the letters in which he recounts this 'randonnée'; sometimes it is no more than a line and a half, but rich as a musical theme.

If you write another preface for another edition and

you would like to make use of some of my reflexions, do so without minding me.

I do not intend to write another preface, but these letters, the value of which Moore felt so well, should I keep them for myself alone? I wrote to him: May I transcribe them? And he replied:

Do what you will with my letters. Transcribe them or burn them. Transcribe them and burn them. Publish them under a phantasy name, under your name or mine. Is it not written somewhere in Molière: *Monsieur, I take my good things wherever I find them.* Let Molière guide and inspire you! One more word, if the letters are published in my name, I hope that here and there you will correct them; I should be delighted with your corrections and take advantage of them without scruples: *I take my good,* etc. etc. . . . My letters were the most rapid improvisation, dictated at conversation speed, and sent as far as I can remember, without being re-read. The suppression, the transposition of a phrase will improve them. Do me this favour, my good sir.

This favour, I am refusing it. I am transcribing the letters as they are, trying to retain the rapidity of the spoken word—the rapidity of that manner of speech which I am sure all those will recognize, who have ever been to the house in Ebury Street, famous for its talk. There one must have seen George Moore, surrounded by his beautiful drawings, prints, pictures of France, he himself speaking of his next novel, and quoting abundantly phrases of Walter Pater or Théophile Gautier. Was it not Hokusai, the great Japanese, who as an octogenerian signed his letters: Hokusai, the old man mad on drawing? George Moore could sign his: George Moore, the old man mad on prose.

From *Pays Parisiens*

241

NOTES ON DEGAS
Written down by Daniel Halévy
1891–1893

This evening, Duhesme[1] and Degas to dinner. Duhesme back from manoeuvres; he speaks of them. Degas, excessively patriotic, does scarcely anything but listen, moreover, Degas likes nothing as much as being silent.

Duhesme gone, Degas talks. At this time he has dealings with house artisans, in connection with the mounting of canes which are his great passion at the moment.[2]

—I should like, he said in this connection, to penetrate into working class families of the Marais. One enters houses which seem ignoble—with doors as wide as this ... And one finds very light rooms, scrupulously clean ... The doors are open onto the landings; all the world is gay, all the world works; nor have these people the servility common to the shopkeepers ... It is a delightful society.

To compare it with a tale that I had already heard and that Degas repeated again this evening. He was in Burgundy, with his friends, the Jeanniots, where he had just arrived by carriage from Paris. Well in the country lived a lady G—— very beautiful and very elegant. This lady knowing him to be in the district invited him to dinner; she is excessively decolleté and slightly astonished at seeing him in a jacket. 'Madame', he said, 'I did not come from Paris in a carriage hired at 10 francs a day to wear dinner dress in the evenings.' They sit down to dinner: Mme

---

[1] General of the cavalry and friend of Ludovic Halévy.

[2] Vollard, then only just 20 years old, had boldly approached Degas, and, as a promising start of his career, arranged to supply Degas with wood from the Antilles, where he was born, in exchange for some drawings.

242

G—— has Degas at her side. Degas cannot stop looking at her shoulders.

'You embarrass me', she said to him.

'I should much like to be able to do otherwise.'

And Degas concludes his little story: 'It was necessary to talk to her as if she were a simple actress.'

Degas also spoke about his plans for work. 'I want to devote myself to drawing for a whole year', he told us.

I have often heard Degas express contempt (relative) for everything in colour. Moreover, he has a particular manner of translating his ideas by gestures. With him the gesture is not a coarse manifestation of his thoughts; Degas when he speaks always involuntarily searches for the ideal line, the curve which will be equal to his thoughts. One day he said to my mother: 'Louise, I should very much like to do your portrait; you are excessively drawn.'[1]

He raged against the management of the Louvre. Recently workmen whilst plastering a vault allowed some plasterwork to fall on the *Pèlerins d'Emmaus*, 'one of the masterpieces of the human mind'.—But then what kind of keepers are there there? Do they love pictures? What is this Kaempfen? A journalist! Oh! *'la gent de lettre!'* as Proudhon said.

And he repeated several times as if to himself *'La gent de Lettre! La gent de Lettre!'*

Afterwards he spoke of old things and of old times, of

[1] Degas told Vollard that if he could have had his own way, he would have confined himself entirely to black and white: 'But if one has the whole world on one's back, which wants colour and colour only! of all my work perhaps some drawings will remain.'
He is also said to have asked Forain to deliver the speech at his funeral saying only this: 'He was very fond of drawing'.

243

superior methods of fabrication which the old closed corporations assured, of the struggle between the corporation of painters and the Academy and in this connection of the admission of painters to the corporation and in particular of Watteau.

In order to be admitted it was necessary to hand in a picture to the jury who after a few days voted and decided. Well, Watteau had not been ready at the appointed time, but only for the actual day of the voting. He did not let a little thing like that disturb him and simply placed his picture in the corridor leading to the voting chamber. The judges arrived, the canvas halted them in the passage and they did not stand on ceremony: Watteau was accepted.

Saying this Degas stretched out his hand; my mother thinking that he was leaving, took it. But he had merely wanted to imply by this gesture the simplicity of this act, its 'graciousness' to use a word the meaning of which he has almost renewed.

Degas was silent a moment after relating this anecdote. 'Today', he added, 'one does not arrive so easily . . . one must pass through the newspapers . . .'

He was silent for another moment, and then very quick and very low: 'You will never see me there . . .'

Cavé who lunched with us this morning had recently been to a cyclists' arena where Degas had asked him to see two dancers from the opera do a comic act on tricycles. And Cavé told us how amusing was Degas' attitude towards these little persons and the attitude of these little persons towards Degas. He finds them quite charming, treats them like his own children, excusing everything

244

they do and laughing at everything they say. They on the other hand have a real veneration for him and the most insignificant little 'rat' would give a great deal to please Degas.

This evening Degas for dinner. He tells us of a remark he made about Jean-Paul Laurens. It was at an exhibition in front of a historic picture; a distracted Merovingian woman is escaping from a house which forms the background of the picture. All very discordant in colour and, on the frame a historical note: A Gunslwinde escapes . . .

'Well!' exclaimed Degas, 'you think you know why this young lady is running away so fast? You know nothing: it is because she does not agree with the background.' 'I think', added Degas, 'that this remark was repeated to Jean-Paul Laurens, because one day I asked a model for whom he was posing, he replied: 'For J-P. Laurens; and as a matter of fact when I told him one day that I was posing for you he made a gesture . . .' as if he had trodden on a serpent, concluded Degas.

At dinner, having just uttered I know not what flippancy, my mother remarked familiarly: 'One must constantly tell you that you are stupid.'

'I don't mind in the least', he replied, 'as long as I always draw a little.'

Thursday 1 Oct. 1891.

DEGAS: Women think in little parcels . . . I cannot understand their mentality at all . . . they make an envelope for each subject, they put a label on it and its finished . . . little parcels . . . little parcels.

DEGAS: I had Forain to dinner the other day. He came to keep me company.

And his wife?

(contemptuously): She was unwell.

It was not true?

Can one say? Women have invented the word 'unwell'; it means nothing at all.

31 Jan. 1892.

After having raged against men of letters, Degas referring to the cutting of diamonds said: 'What a delightful thing is the conversation of specialists! One understands absolutely nothing and it's charming. Haas told me that he was once a member of an art commission where two mathematicians were present; he was sitting in front of them and, being very bored, he listened to them. They were speaking of the present state of mathematics and one of them said: 'You see, the square of the hypotenuse will always be young'.

That reminds me of a remark by another mathematician. He was turning over the pages of a volume on algebra by Lermite and looking at the pages covered with figures. 'One can always recognize at once a page by Lermite', he said.

Canderax recently wrote an article in which he mentioned Degas; and Degas, with his habitual sweetness, had been irritated by it. Ganderax knew this and wrote a letter of apology; Degas replied rather stiffly: 'In future do not irritate me any more'. My father teased him a little about his mania and quoted some rather fine words of Mounet-Sully: 'You speak too low, one can scarcely hear you', said the director of the Théâtre Français.—'Am I playing for them? Let them buy the text and follow it. I act as I should.' And as Claretie was complaining at having to rehearse one piece of the repertoire five times: 'Monsieur l'administrateur, let me tell you that one should always rehearse'.

'That is what you think', said my mother.

'No, I think one should work for a few people, as for the others it is quite immaterial.

Thursday 12 Feb. 1892.

Degas also told us this anecdote about Barbey d'Aurevilly, the writer, and Mlle Read.[1]

X . . . was at Barbey's one morning. It was 9 o'clock, Mlle Read was not there. She came in: 'Mademoiselle', said Barbey d'Aurevilly to her, 'I should like to know what I can count on. Are you nursing me, are you not nursing me? If you are nursing me come earlier! If you are not nursing me go away.' Mlle Read went out without replying and in the next room cleaned, tidied and dusted. 'Learn, young man', said Barbey d'Aurevilly in his stertorian voice, 'the secret of being loved. 'X . . . a little revolted went out and before leaving said to Mlle Read that it was really very good of her to nurse such a stupid man. 'When we are alone', she replied, 'he is charming . . .'

Saturday 14 Feb. 1892.

DEGAS: 'At last I shall be able to devote myself to black and white, which is my passion.'

Thursday 19 Feb. 1892.

Degas tells us that Mallarmé came to see him the other day on behalf of Roujon, the new director of the Beaux

---

[1] In 1893 Mlle Read had lost her young brother whose first poems had been very much admired. Inconsolable at the loss, she devoted the rest of her life—forty years—to helping poor writers.

247

Arts, to sound him and find out, if he would consent to give a picture to the Luxembourg. He told us how he received these advances: in a fine manner!

'I told him, most certainly not, of course. These people want to make me think that I have "arrived". "Arrived", what does that mean? One has always done so and never —arrived at what? It means hanging on a wall next to a lady by Bouguereau and the *Slave Market* by Toto Girod? I want none of it. When everyone pulls his own way and attracts his own little public, what do the committees want to stick their noses into it for? I pay them my contributions, are my pictures any of their business? But no! They have to have a finger in every pie! They have the chess board of the Fine Arts on their table and we, the artists, we are the pawns . . . They move this pawn here, that pawn there . . . I am not a pawn, I do not want to be moved!'

My father grew angry and called him an imbecile: 'Do you know what you seem like? An embittered man, who thinks he is being approached too late!'

'Embittered? But I am very pleased. Everyone knows that.'

'Those who know you'.

'You do not see that in the higher sense. The fact is that if I were to become a member of the Luxembourg I should imagine I were being led to the guard-room! Arrived! One remains stationary! Arrived! What does that mean? Does one ever arrive?[1] I do not wish to be seized by the policemen of the Beaux Arts, or by that officer of the peace known as Roujon . . .'

---

[1] 'In my day', Degas used to say to a friend, 'one never arrived.'

Monday 27 Feb. 1892.

Degas came to join us at lunch the other day as jolly as a sand-boy. He was delighted at the show of discord amongst the painters which always followed after the Salon. The misery of Boldini, the pride of Helleu because Mirbeau mentioned the one and not the other delighted him. My father then seized this opportunity to tell him that Roujon was annoyed because he went about everywhere defaming him. 'I saw him', my father said, 'and he spoke rather bitterly to me, saying that he saw nothing very criminal in having asked you for a picture. I told him that you were always like that and that you were only joking. But I shall take you to the opera once when Roujon is there and I shall introduce you.'

'I want nothing better', replied Degas. 'But I do not want you to defend me as you do, by saying that I am an old lunatic. You must say I am a philosopher. Not a lunatic but a philosopher, an old philosopher. Tell him: 'They think that he is original; if you were to start a discussion with him he would make you quiet in two words: he is a...'

It was the word 'philosopher' that he wanted to repeat, but he was laughing so much that he could not speak. Well, the same morning he had had to send back a letter that he had received and was unable to read, so bad was his sight growing. He told us that without a shadow of sadness and I had never seen him so gay. That was only the pride of a man who does not wish to be an object of pity and who wishes to find in himself the strength to live joyously. He knows, without doubt, that in two years he will be blind: Degas is not the man to have any illu-

249

sions or to hide the truth from himself. But the sadness he does not express, assuredly has a lot to do with the present violence of his recluse tendencies.

Degas came to dinner, to the country, this summer. The conversation turned to Lourdes. Elie[1] came back full of anger which was easily shared by my grandmother and my aunt:

'Lourdes! Yes, I have been there', said Degas.[2] And as he said no more, the others urged him. Elie said: 'It's ignoble'.

'Ignoble? Heavens, I saw a little of everything. There were women there who sang with remarkable exaltation; there were others who were as calm as in their shops, and others who acted a part. I saw the bearers. I saw one young bearer who was drinking in a pub with a bored expression, and who must have been thinking: Three more patients or my aunt will give me nothing next month. And then I saw bearers convinced by their miracles. I saw a little of everything.' They pressed him still further. But these miracles! In a word! Ignominous!

'Well!' replied Degas. 'Why! There is nothing absurd in it.'

There was laughter as at some amusing paradox.

'If one were to tell me: Here is a bottle. Put it over your tummy for five minutes and you will have a good life for a hundred years. I should put it there. What? Everything is possible.' He became excited: 'Reason! You are going to speak of reason! What does that mean? Nothing has caused more nonsense to be said than reason; one should not use it, or at the most only as an instrument for getting on to an omnibus.

[1] Son of Ludovic Halévy.   [2] See letter, No. 136.

'But', said my grandmother, 'if it were said of you tomorrow that you have lost your reason, would you like that?'

'That would not stop me from doing a good drawing'.

Sept. 1892

Degas came to dinner yesterday with his niece, a young American girl who is living with him, and whom he invited on condition that she should never ask him to be her escort. And sure enough this young girl roams round Paris from morning to night; after dinner, Degas takes her to the theatre, but never anywhere but the Batignolles, Moncey or Montmarte.[1]

After dinner the conversation turned to the Arabian Nights, and Degas asked me if I had heard anything about the English edition I was to enquire about. I told him: '15 volumes and 900 francs.'

'I imagined 1200', replied Degas. And he added: 'You are going to buy it?' We all cried out.—'But why not?' What are you thinking of, 900 francs!—'900 francs, what is that to you? What does money mean? Does it exist? What does exist is my desire. Money! Money! and after that? I tell you what, I shall buy the translation, with my own money, 900 francs. What is that to me? I shall do a pastel or two or three more and it will do the trick. I shall pay them these 900 francs, and then, at my place, I shall look at my 15 volumes, and I shall be delighted! delighted! And then you will see me arriving here with a volume under one arm, and you will read a little of it to me. I

[1] At Batignolles and Montmartre there were romantic melodramas; at Moncey comic operas, both Italian and French, of the first half of the nineteenth century.

251

shall have them, I shall have them, and the best of it is that I shall not be able to read them.'

At that moment he would have bought them. He told Elie to find them for him as a bargain in London, which calmed him a little.

'And then', he said, 'I can pay for them. I have 21 landscapes.'

We all cried out: '21 landscapes? Degas had never done any; 21 landscapes?'

'Why, yes! 21 landscapes'.[1]

'But what does it mean?'

'The fruits of my journeys this summer. I stood at the doors of the coaches and I looked round vaguely. That gave me the idea to do the landscapes. There are 21 of them.'

'What? Very vague things?'

'Perhaps'.

'States of the mind?' said my father. Amiel said: 'A landscape is a state of mind. Do you like the phrase?'

'State of the eyes', replied Degas, 'we do not use such pretentious language.'[2]

Oct. 1892

Degas came but little this winter. Did he see his other friends more? I think that at the moment he is keeping

[1] These landscapes were exhibited in the Durand-Ruel galleries in October 1892. (See Pissarro, letters to his son Lucien, ed. John Rewald, 2 Oct. 1892.)

[2] Degas persevered for some weeks in this new career. He had his own methods of creating landscapes. At that moment the rue Victor-Massé, which he passed every day on his way from his home to the studio, was being repaired. He used to pick up stone splinters, the shapes of which he thought superb. He baptized one of them 'Le Cap de la belle Epaule' (the cape of the beautiful shoulder).

very much to himself. His eyes are getting worse and worse and he wears special glasses which embarrass him very much; all that saddens him and I suspect he remains alone to hide from our eyes the melancholia against which he has striven so hard.

Last month he must have stopped work completely to get accustomed to his new glasses. He went all alone to Belgium for a week, without reading a single word, not even the railway guides.

April 1893.

DEGAS: 'Today I was at the Champs de Mars with Zandomeneghi known as the Prince, Mangin, Cammondo and Mlle Salles, Bartholomé.'

'And the Walkyrie? Did they talk about the rehearsal of the Walkyrie?'

'Oh, oh! they wanted to at lunch. But Zandomeneghi known as the Prince was there who had just heard the *Secret Mariage* at Bologna, Manzi was there, and we said: "It's not all that good". And we started to sing; the others insulted us, but we went on all the time: "La la la—la la la—Lalalalala. And they fell upon us." '1

---

1 Degas was not unappreciative of the beauty of Wagner, but he did not wish to addict himself to it. This was the same for Beethoven. I have heard him say to a young woman who had sat down at the piano to entertain him and was starting a Beethoven sonata: 'When I hear Beethoven, it seems to me that I am walking in a forest, alone and bowed down with all my sorrows. Play me Mozart or Gluck.' From his Neapolitan youth he had retained a love of old Italian music. Today it is hard for us to appreciate the scandal caused by the three singers of Cimarosa. It is a matter of fifty years since old Italian music was reinstated honourably. At the time of which we are speaking, fascinated by the one and only Wagner, it was totally discredited.

LIST OF ILLUSTRATIONS

6. MME JULIE BURTIN. 1863
Pencil on white paper. $14'' \times 10''$.
Fogg Museum of Art (Paul J. Sachs Coll.),
Cambridge, Mass.

7. MOUNTED JOCKEY. 1866
Brush drawing a l'essence heighted with white,
on brown paper. $10'' \times 5''$.
Fogg Museum of Art (Paul J. Sachs Coll.),
Cambridge, Mass.

8. MME HERTEL. 1865
Pencil on white paper. $14\frac{1}{8}'' \times 9''$.
Fogg Museum of Art (Paul J. Sachs Coll.),
Cambridge, Mass.
*Study for the painting 'La femme aux chrysan-
thèmes'.*

9. WOMAN WITH CRYSANTHEMUMS. MME
HERTEL. 1865
Oil on canvas. $29\frac{1}{8}'' \times 36\frac{1}{4}''$.
The Metropolitan Museum of Art, New York
(H. O. Havemeyer Coll.).

10. SELF-PORTRAIT
Pencil.
Coll. Nepveu De Gas.
Photo Marcel Guérin.

11. EDOUARD MANET. 1864
Pencil on white paper. $14\frac{1}{8}'' \times 9''$.
Fogg Museum of Art (Paul J. Sachs Coll.),
Cambridge, Mass.
Study for the etchings of Manet.

12. SELF-PORTRAIT. About 1857
    Oil on canvas. $9'' \times 7''$.
    Coll. J. Bomford, Laines.

13. BALLET DANCERS. 1876–77
    Left half of a drawing in sepia with touches of
        blue ink.
    Size of the complete sheet $7\frac{3}{4}'' \times 9\frac{3}{4}''$.
    Fogg Museum of Art (Paul J. Sachs Coll.),
        Cambridge, Mass.

14. THE BALLET MASTER. 1875
    Sketch a l'essence on greenish grey paper.
        $18\frac{3}{4}'' \times 11\frac{3}{4}''$.
    Coll. Henry P. McIlhenny, Philadelphia.
    *Study for the two paintings entitled 'La Classe de
        Danse' in the Louvre (Camondo Bequest) and in
        Coll. Harry P. Bingham, New York.*

15. SELF-PORTRAIT
    Pencil.
    Photo Marcel Guérin.
    *Study for the portrait of Degas and de Valernes in
        the Louvre.*

16. DIEGO MARTELLI. 1879
    Black crayon with touches of white chalk on
        grey-brown paper. $17\frac{3}{4}'' \times 11\frac{1}{2}''$.
    Fogg Museum of Art (Paul J. Sachs Coll.),
        Cambridge, Mass.
    Study for the painting of Diego Martelli.

17. DIEGO MARTELLI. 1879
    Oil on canvas. $29\frac{1}{2}'' \times 45\frac{1}{4}''$.
    Museo Nacional de Bellas Artes, Buenos Aires.
    Photo Jacques Seligmann and Co., New York.

256

18. MISS CASSATT AT THE LOUVRE. 1880
Pastel on gray paper. $23\frac{1}{2}'' \times 18\frac{1}{2}''$.
Signed upper right and dedicated: à mes amis
Bartholomé.
Coll. Henry P. McIlhenny, Philadelphia.

19. MISS CASSATT AT THE LOUVRE. 1880
Pencil on white paper. $13\frac{1}{2}'' \times 10\frac{1}{2}''$.
Private Coll., London.
Photo Dr. Kauffmann, London.
Study for the engraving Delteil, no. 30.

20. TWO FEMALE NUDES, STUDIES FOR
DANCERS
Pencil on white paper. $10'' \times 15\frac{1}{2}''$.
Coll. Grete Ring, London.

21. BALLET DANCER
Black pencil heightened with white chalk.
$17\frac{3}{4}'' \times 11''$.
Photo Leicester Galleries, London.
*Study for the painting 'Dancer at the Photographer',
Museum of Modern Art, Moscow.*

22. BALLET DANCER
Indian ink heightened with gouache.
$25\frac{1}{4}'' \times 19\frac{1}{4}''$.
Photo Leicester Galleries, London.

23. BALLET DANCER
Pencil. $18'' \times 11\frac{3}{4}''$.
Private Coll. Switzerland.
Photo Paul Cassirer Ltd.

24. BALLET DANCER
Charcoal. $16'' \times 20''$.
Coll. E. Schwabe, Manchester.
Photo Gallery Mathiessen, London.

25. THE COIFFURE
Charcoal heightened with pastel. $23\frac{1}{2}'' \times 16\frac{3}{8}''$.
Photo Durand-Ruel, Paris.

26. BALLET DANCER
Oil. $15\frac{3}{4}'' \times 12\frac{1}{2}''$.
Formerly Coll. Viau, Paris.
Photo Paul Cassirer Ltd.

27. BALLET-REHEARSAL. About 1910
Canvas. $29\frac{1}{4}'' \times 31\frac{3}{4}''$.
Photo Alex. Reid and Lefevre, London.

On the Cover:

YOUTH BLOWING A TRUMPET
Detail of a drawing in the Coll. Grete Ring, London.

258

ANNOTATIONS

LETTER 1

1. JAQUES JOSEPH TISSOT was born at Nantes in 1836; he studied in Paris under Lamothe, Flandrin and Ingres and developed a friendship with Whistler and Degas who painted his portrait (now in the Metropolitan Museum in New York). His sketches made during the siege of Paris in 1870, in which he took part, were published as illustrations to the letters of his friend Thomas Gibson Bowles, editor of *Vanity Fair*. As a member of the Commune he had to leave Paris in 1871 and went to London where he soon became famous for the elegance of his pictures which fetched very high prices. Agnew for instance paid Gns. 1200 for the *Concert*, which is now in Manchester. He intended to remain in England, but a scandal caused by the suicide of a lady with whom he had formed an intimate friendship forced him to leave the country. When he returned to Paris Degas, who in the meantime had learned about his communard activities in 1871, refused to see him. (Cf. James Laver, The romantic career of James Tissot. Constable, London 1936.)

The eight letters to James Tissot were acquired by the Bibliothèque Nationale in Paris from a sale at the Hôtel Drouot in March 1946 for frcs. 66,200.

2. 'The affliction of a blind spot made the later half of Degas' life a perpetual and tormenting exercise of circumvention. He told me that he attributed this affliction to the fact that, during the siege of Paris, he had slept in a studio with a high window from which the cold air poured down on his face at night. . . .

It was natural that, during the years when I knew him, from '83 onwards, he should sometimes have spoken of the torment that it was to draw, when he could only see around the spot at which he was looking, and never the spot itself. When we consider the immense output of the later half of his life, the high intellectual value of it, and the generous store of beauty that forms its contribution to the history of art, the debonair heroism of such a life, its inspired adaptation to conditions apparently intolerable, must remain a monument for amazement and for respect.

It may safely be said that the curious and unique development of the art of pastel that this obstacle compelled him to evolve would not have come into being but for his affliction. A larger scale became a necessity. For the shiny medium of oil-paint was substituted the flat one of pastel. Minute delicacies of detailed execution had to be abandoned. A very natural dread that the affliction might grow made, of the necessary delays that oil-painting exacts, an intolerable anxiety. A pastel is always ready to be gone on with.

I don't know that it is necessary to hold a brief for the one or the other period. Rather is it interesting to understand their growth and the relation of each to the other. I find a peculiar satisfaction in recognizing that this giant among the moderns founded his art on the old traditions of oil-painting, on the rich and glowing colour of transparent shadows and on delicate and exquisite impasto in the lights. That the immortal gods, as Homer assured us, though their residences may be distant, are on excellent terms with each other.'

WALTER SICKERT

From the Burlington Magazine, 43, 1923, *p.* 308

LETTER 2

On the notepaper the printed heading DE GAS BROTHERS, NEW ORLEANS and in Degas' handwriting: Thanking you for your kind remembrance. The real family name was written in two words. It was the painter who first signed his name in one word. Only his earliest drawings are signed De Gas.

DÉSIRÉ DIHAU, Bassoonist in the orchestra of the Parisian opera, was an intimate friend of Degas who represented him in the centre of his painting *l'Orchestre de l'Opéra*, now in the Louvre. Some of the songs which he composed were published with lithos by Toulouse-Lautrec whose cousin he was. His sister, Mlle Marie Dihau, was an excellent musician. Degas who had a certain affection for her, painted two portraits of her. One which is now in the Louvre represents her sitting in front of her piano. Marcel Guérin tells her story: When I made her acquaintance she was a charming old lady, a spinster, living alone in a modest apartment. She had a small income and gave singing lessons—often free— to young Montmartre girls who were preparing to be singers in cafés. All round her she kept her relics of the past, and what relics: they included the picture *l'Orchestre* by Degas, her portraits by Degas and Toulouse-Lautrec and the portraits of her brothers by Lautrec. One little portrait by Degas which shows her seated at a table with her travelling bag beside her was bought from her by Durand Ruel and sold to America. But although badly in need of money as a result of the Russian revolution she did not want to part with the other one, which shows her at the piano, or with the *Orchestre*. So together with my friend M. David-Weill, president of the National Museums' Council, I arranged to pay her a life annuity

260

of 12000 frs. in exchange for the two pictures which were to belong to us after her death. As a result of the Degas exhibition which we organised in 1924 and where these two pictures, exhibited for the first time, caused a sensation, the Louvre asked us to hand our contract with Mlle Dihau over to them. In this way the pictures became the property of the Louvre.

LETTER 10

The famous singer FAURE was one of the first to buy pictures by Manet and Degas. He acquired Manet's *Bon Bock*, now in the National Gallery, for 6.000 frs. and Degas' *Carriage at the Races*, now in the Museum of Fine Arts in Boston, for 1.500 frs. from Durand Ruel. In 1872 he commissioned Degas to paint a picture of an examination or dance class at the Opera (today in the Payne collection in New York). Degas delivered it to Faure in 1874 at the price of 5.000 frs.— a high one for those days.

At the same time Degas told Faure that he did not want to leave certain of his pictures at Durand-Ruel's for sale, as he wished to make some alterations. Accordingly Faure bought these pictures from Durand-Ruel for 8.000 frs. They were: *L'Orchestre, Le Banquier, Cheveux au pré, Sortie du pesage, Les Musiciens, La Blanchisseuse*. Faure paid Degas an additional sum of 1.500 frs. and returned the pictures to Degas who in exchange was to give him four large pictures, well advanced at the time, *Les Danseuses Roses, L'Orchestre de Robert le Diable, Grand Champ de Courses, Les Grandes Blanchisseuses*. The first two were delivered by Degas in 1876. (Robert le Diable is today in the South Kensington Museum.) When the other two were still not ready in 1887, Faure lost patience and filed a suit against Degas. As a result Degas had to deliver the pictures.

LETTER 11

This first EXHIBITION took place in 1874 at 35 Boulevard des Capucines. The following artists exhibited: Astruc, Attendu, Béliard, Boudin, Bracquemond, Brandon, Bureau, Cals, Cézanne, Colin, Desbras, Degas, Guillaumin, Latouche, Lepic, Lépine, Levert, Meyer, de Molins, Monet, Mulot-Durivage, de Nittis, Ottin (Auguste), Ottin (Léon), Pissarro, Renoir, Rouart, Robert (Léopold), Sisley.

Manet had refused to take part. He was only interested in the *Salon* and never exhibited at any exhibition of the Impressionists. Degas showed two *Répétitions de Danse*, one of which is now in the Louvre (Camondo Bequest), an *Intérieure de Coulisse*, which was sold for 400.000 frs. at the Vente Rouart in 1912, and the *Courses en Provence*. Renoir showed *La Petite Danseuse* and the *Loge*. One of

Manet's pictures bore the title *Impression*, whence the name Impressionists given to the whole. Not till the third exhibition in 1877, however, did the exhibitors accept the name and the same year their friend Georges Rivière founded the journal *L'Impressionisme*.

The relations between Degas and Manet were not always good. Degas admired Manet very much but did not always show it and that irritated Manet. At one point the two great artists quarrelled because Manet had cut in two a portrait that Degas had done of Manet and his wife.

Degas told Vollard the story: 'Would you believe, that Manet did that? He thought that Mme Manet was not good enough. Well, I shall try to restore her. But can you imagine what I felt, when I saw my sketch in Manet's studio? Without wasting a word I left with the picture under my arm. At home I took from the wall a little still-life which he had once given me: 'Dear Sir,' I wrote, 'I return herewith your *Plums*.'

Later on they became friends again—'how can one be angry with Manet for long'—and Degas regretted his hastiness: 'After all perhaps Manet was right. And the plums! Ah! How lovely that canvas was! I did a bad deal that day because later, after Manet and I had made it up, I asked to have the plums back. Well, he had sold them.'

LETTER 38

Louis Emile Edmond Duranty, 1833–1880, author and critic, one of the leading representatives of the realist movement. In 1876 he published a very important booklet entitled: *La Nouvelle Peinture, à propos du groupe d'artistes qui expose dans les galeries Durand-Ruel.* (New Edition by Marcel Guérin at the Librairie Floury.) He does not mention any names, but it is easy to recognize Fromentin, Gustave Moreau, Legros, Fantin, Whistler, Jongkind, Boudin, Stevens, Bracquemond, Claude Monet, and finally Degas.

The following passage obviously refers to Degas: 'This series of new ideas was formed in the first place in the mind of a draftsman, one of our own kind, one of those who exhibit in these rooms, a man of the rarest talent and intelligence.

The idea, the first idea, was to break down the barriers which separated the studio from ordinary life, which shocks the writer in the *Revue des Deux Mondes* (Fromentin). It was necessary to draw the artist out of his shell, out of his seclusion where he communes only with the heavens and to bring him back amongst men, into the world.

Later he was shown, what he had previously ignored, that our life is spent in rooms or in the street, and that rooms and the street have their special laws of light and expression.'

After Duranty's death a sale was organised. In the introduction to the catalogue Zola appealed to all friends to help Duranty's penniless widow. Degas responded to the appeal, but prices were low: a drawing touched up with pastel, a study for the famous Duranty portrait, fetched 500 frs; a sketch on oil paper, *Femme regardant avec une Lorgnette*, only 100 frs.; a dancer in pastel, 550 frs. and a black and white sketch of a Dancer, 60 frs.

Degas painted Duranty's portrait in 1879 (I Sale no. 48, sold for 79.000 frs.); a portrait drawing is now in the Fogg Museum in Cambridge, Mass.

LETTER 40A

ALFRED GREVIN, 1827–1892, founder of the wax work exhibition in Paris, was also a celebrated draftsman and caricaturist, who created a specialised genre—the humorous caricature without pretention to ethics or philosophy. A much esteemed designer of theatrical costumes he contributed to no less than 65 plays, operas, operettes and ballets—that was probably a link between him and Degas. In 1881, the year of this letter, he did 400 drawings for a book by Pierre Véron, called *La Chaire Des Dames* in the series *Paris Vicieux*. It is, perhaps, to this that Degas here refers. (Prof. Turquet)

LETTER 40B

The letter refers to the sonnet:

Petite Danseuse

Danse, gamin ailé, sur les gazons de bois:
N'aime rien que ça, danseuse pour la vie.
Ton bras mince, placé dans la ligne suivie,
Equilibre, balance et ton vol, et ton poids.

Taglioni, venez, princesse d'Arcadie,
Nymphes, Graces, venez des cimes d'autrefois,
Ennoblir et former, souriant de mon choix,
Le petit être neuf, à la mine hardie.

Si Montmartre a donné l'esprit et les aïeux, ·
Roxelane le nez, et la Chine les yeux,
Attentif Ariel, donne à cette recrue

Tes pas légers de jour, tes pas légers de nuit;
Fais que, pour mon plaisir, elle sente son fruit
Et garde, aux palais d'or, la race de sa rue.

Little Dancer

Dance, wingéd child, in your stage built glade.
Dance be your life, dance be your charm.
In its sinuous line, let your slender arm
Gracefully balance your glide and your weight.

Taglioni awake! Come Arcady's queen!
Nymphs, graces, descend from your far off height;
With a smile at my choice, imbue with your light
That creature so new, so gallant of mien.

If Montmartre gave the forebears, the spirit so wise,
Roxelane the nose and China the eyes,
Hearken, oh Ariel, give this young fay

The lightness, by day and by night, of your feet
And see, for my sake, in her golden palais,
She remembers her race, her descent from the street.

There exist some 20 sonnets by Degas. (New Edition by Marcel Guérin). Their subjects are mostly similar to those of his paintings.

One day when he was dining with Mallarmé at Berthe Morisot's house Degas complained about the extreme difficulty of writing poetry: 'What a profession,' he exclaimed. 'I have wasted the whole day on a damned sonnet without progressing one step. Not that I have not got enough ideas! I am full of them, I have too many. . . .' Mallarmé, in his quiet way, replied: 'One does not write poetry with ideas, Degas, but with words.' (Paul Valery, in *Degas, Danse, Dessin*, Gallimard 1938.) The wax statuette of a young dancer was exhibited by Degas at the exhibitions in 1880 and 1881.

LETTER 41

Degas did several etchings with crayon electrique (carbon): *Ellen Andrée* (Delteil no. 20), *Danseuse entre des portants* (D.23), *Miss Cassatt au Louvre* (D.29, 30), *Cabinet de toilette* (D.34) and especially *Sortie du Bain* (D.39) which is probably the one referred to in this letter. One evening after Degas had dined at the house of Alexis Rouart, Boulevard Voltaire, he was prevented from returning home by a storm and slept at Rouart's house. The next morning he asked for a copper plate: 'I want to make an etching,' he said. In Rouart's kitchen a copper plate was found, on which Degas engraved *La Sortie du Bain* with a pencil made from the carbon of an electric lamp.

264

LETTER 46

COUNT LEPIC besides being a great dog breeder was also a painter and engraver. He had taught Degas how to do monotypes, some of which are signed by both Lepic and Degas. Degas represented Lepic several times: in the famous painting of the Place de la Concorde, where he walks behind his two little daughters, then in the picture where he sits behind Marcellin Desboutin (I Sale no. 11, now in the Louvre) and in a pastel (III Sale no. 87, formerly collection Viau).

LETTER 99

Degas was never satisfied with his pictures and often tried to recover them in order to improve some details, sometimes with fatal results for the pictures. When the German painter Max Liebermann visited him in Paris he remarked: 'I would like to be rich enough to buy back all my pictures and destroy them by pushing my foot through the canvas.' (Quoted by Karl Scheffler, Die fetten und die mageren Jahre, Leipzig 1946.)

When Vollard suggested that he should have one of his little wax statues cast in bronze he refused and destroyed it. Noticing Vollard's disappointment he said: 'You are thinking of its money value only! But even a hat full of diamonds would not make me as happy as I was to destroy it—for all the pleasure I shall have in remodelling it.'

LETTER 114

Vollard, in his memoirs, recalls a visit to Degas at Rouart's country house. He found him in a little room, painting a landscape, with his back to the window. Noticing Vollard's astonishment he said: 'On a journey, from time to time, I put my nose out of the carriage window. One does not even have to leave one's room. A green pea soup with three old wooden paint brushes in it is enough material to paint all the landscapes in the world. The other day Rouart painted a water colour at the edge of a precipice. Is painting, then, a sport?'

Vollard: 'When I walked along the Boulevard Clichy the other day, I saw a horse in the air, being hoisted on a rope into a painter's studio.' Degas took a little wooden horse from a table and said: 'When I come back from the races these are my models; how would it be possible to turn real horses so as to get the right light?'

About one of the Impressionist exhibitions at Durand Ruel's gallery he said: 'I met Monet there: "I am leaving," I told him. "All these reflections on the water make my eyes ache" . . . and then I had the feeling that there was such a draught in the exhibition. Very nearly turned up my collar!'

265

'But what if you want to paint a scene in the open, as for instance beach in the collection Rouart?' somebody asked.

Degas: 'That is easy. I spread my flannel coat on the floor in my studio and make the model sit on it. You see, the air which one breathes in a picture is different to that outside.'

It is significant that in his collection Degas had paintings by Sisley, Renoir, Berthe Morisot and Guillaumin, but none by Monet.

Berthe Morisot notes in her diary: 'Degas said that the study of nature is unimportant because painting is a conventional art and it would be infinitely better to learn drawing from Holbein. (Paul Valéry in *Degas, Danse, Dessin*, Gallimard 1938.)

LETTER 121

1. MANZI, born in Naples in 1849, officer in the Italian artillery, entered the Paris printing firm of Goupil in 1881. He specialised in printing collotype and chromotype-gravure and besides was a remarkable draftsman. His portraits of Degas and the art-collector de Groult are most able and amusing. In 1890 he published a famous portfolio with reproductions of Degas' drawings and pastels. He was on intimate terms with Degas, Manet, Carrière and Toulouse-Lautrec. Both Degas and Lautrec painted his portrait. Together with Maurice Joyant, Lautrec's friend and biographer, he collected Japanese works of art and most of the Japanese prints in the collection Camondo in the Louvre were brought together by them. Later they opened an art gallery in the Rue de la ville L'Evesque and published the periodical *Les Arts* (1910–1913). Manzi died in 1915 and his collections were dispersed at three sales in 1919.

2. CHARLES HAAS was born in 1832 of Jewish parentage. He was one of the most mondaine, brilliant and best known personalities of the period; a friend of all the most influential men of Parisian high society he owed his position to his wit, his elegance, his success with women, his good taste and his artistic knowledge, which made him the disinterested adviser of his society friends. Certain features of Haas were given by Proust to his Swann (*La Prisonière I*, 273). J. Tissot represented him in one of his pictures. Sarah Bernhardt mentioned him in her memoires as 'a man of distinction and charm.'

The fulfilment of his social ambition, the dream of his life came in 1871, after the war in which his courage had been conspicuous, when he was elected member of the Jockey Club from which normally Jews were excluded. He was converted and died an ardent Catholic in 1902. Degas made his acquaintance at Mme Howlands; Haas interested him but he scarcely liked him. 'That Haas,' he used to say, 'what a social climber!' But see letter 180.

266

LETTER 129

MME STRAUS (correct spelling), daughter of Fromental Halévy. Her first husband was George Bizet, the composer of *Carmen*. She was a great beauty and had a famous salon. Degas, who had come to take a pleasure in it, often accompanied her to her tailor's for fittings. One day, astonished at his interest, she asked him what pleased him so much in that. Degas gave this whimsical reply: 'The red hands of the little girl who holds the pins.'

LETTER 168

EVARISTE BERNHARDI DE VALERNES was born in 1820 at the village of Monieux in a little Louis XIII château. He worked in Delacroix's studio and copied a great deal in the Louvre, where he met Manet, Fantin-Latour and Degas. Although he was 14 years older than Degas a firm bond of friendship existed between them. Degas appears to have had a great fondness, almost affection for him. Under the influence of Degas' art this romantic minded man gave up historical for contemporary subjects. He painted a *Malade*, some *Modistes* or *Fleuristes*, and in the museum at Carpentras there is a little study of a dancer on which he has written: 'Study, scarcely begun, of a dancer at the Opera, done in my friend Degas' studio, rue Laval.' In the same studio, Degas painted a portrait of de Valernes, bareheaded, sitting down (Exhibition 1924, no. 27), and another portrait of him with a top hat, seated next to Degas, who is bareheaded and has his chin in his hand. (Now in the Louvre. See M. Guérin, dix neuf portraits de Degas par lui même—Paris 1931.)

De Valernes, who had inherited a rich property, died ruined and unhappy. It is said that Degas, on a visit to Carpentras about 1893, bought back for 3.000 francs the portrait that he had once given him. This portrait was sold for 1.410.000 frs. at the Viau sale in December 1942. (From J. L. Vaudoyer, *Beautés de la Provence*, Paris, Grasset, 1926.)

267

LIST OF RECIPIENTS

Figures refer to numbers of letters

SOURCES

Letter 4: Published by Léo Swane in *Kunstmuseetz Aarsskrift*, 1919.

Letter 26, 28, 70: *L'Amour de l'Art*, July, 1931.

Letter 45, 247: Collection Marc Loliée.

Letter 57, 63: *Revue de France*, 15th March, 1931. *Souvenirs anecdotiques sur Degas* by Jeanne Raunay.

Letter 64, most of the letters to Durand Ruel and 117: Lionello Venturi, *Archives de l'Impressionisme*, Paris, Durand Ruel, 1939.

Letter 195: For the letters to Suzanne Valadon, see Robert Rey, *Suzanne Valadon*, Paris 1922; and Tabarant, *Bulletin de la Vie Artistique*, 15 December 1921. Some of the letters were supplied by John Rewald.

ACKNOWLEDGMENT

THE Publishers desire to express their gratitude to all those who have helped in the preparation of this volume by permitting the reproduction of originals or photographs in their possession and by cooperating in the interpretation of difficult passages: J. Bomford; Sir Louis Fergusson, K.C.V.O.; Sir Gerald Kelly, R.A.; Dr. A. Kauffman; W. K. Loveridge; Henry P. McIlhenny; J. Rewald; Grete Ring; Prof. Paul J. Sachs; E. Schwabe; Prof. Turquet; The Metropolitan Museum of Art, New York; Museo Nacional de Bellas Artes, Buenos Aires; Messrs. Paul Cassirer Ltd; Messrs. Durand-Ruel; The Leicester Galleries; Gallery Matthiesen; Messrs. A. Reid and Lefevre; Messrs. Jacques Seligmann & Co.